Praise for *The Art of Leading Change*

"The Art of Leading Change is a tour-de-force of leadership wisdom and demonstrates why Mike Bonem is a trusted advisor to leaders all over the nation. With creativity and humility, honesty and candor, Bonem brings together decades of leadership wisdom and memorable maxims for navigating the most delicate part of the change process—the *art* of leading people through it. Mike's ten perspectives on the art of leading change will become as cherished to readers as Mike's own coaching is to leaders."

—Todd Bolsinger, author of *Tempered Resilience: How Leaders Are Formed in the Crucible of Change* and *Canoeing the Mountains: Christian Leadership in Uncharted Territory*

"In *The Art of Leading Change* Mike Bonem opens leadership up as an aesthetic act. Like art, leadership is messy, each element a conversation between a tightly woven organizational culture and the brush strokes of meetings and conversations. He challenges us to dig deep and balance that by taking a step back to consider the work underway. This book offers solid advice for both the right- and left-brain leader."

—Rt. Rev. C. Andrew Doyle, the Episcopal Bishop of the Diocese of Texas, and author of *Citizen* and *Embodied Liturgy*

"I'm not sure there is a more important book coming out of a world-wide pandemic and an intense season of political and spiritual unrest. Get ready to mark up every page. Few leadership books on change must be read by everyone in a position of influence. This one is on that list. Read it as soon as possible."

—Judy West, pastor of staff & leadership development at The Crossing, St. Louis MO, and leader of WXP, an international group of Women Executive Pastors

"The need to navigate massive change is a crucial competency for spiritual leaders. Especially now with the church's critical need to move from church-as-institution to church-as-movement. I am glad that Mike Bonem has decided to distill and distribute his many practical suggestions about how this is done in *The Art of Leading Change*. I can't imagine a ministry team that would not be helped by processing this book together."

—REGGIE MCNEAL, best-selling author of
Kingdom Come and *Kingdom Collaborators*

"In *The Art of Leading Change*, Mike Bonem hits a brilliant balance of the complexity *and* potential for leading change today. He masterfully draws from the wisdom of family systems theory and organizational dynamics along with his own insights from years of experience with congregations to produce actionable guidance for navigating change. In a season that can feel overwhelming for leaders in the church, this book offers practical handholds. As I read it, I found myself feeling genuinely hopeful."

—LISA GREENWOOD, vice president for
leadership ministry, Wesleyan Investive and
Texas Methodist Foundation (TMF).

"Leading change is never easy, and it's not an option. Mike Bonem offers invaluable insights on how to better understand and practice the art of leading people through change. Throughout this book, you will find deep thought, helpful stories, biblical foundations, and perhaps some of the best wisdom and advice you can receive on leading change."

—DAN REILAND, executive pastor, 12Stone Church,
Lawrenceville, GA, and author of *Confident Leader!*

"He's done it again. I had the privilege of working with Mike on a couple of his titles while I was at Leadership Network. This new book, *The Art of Leading Change*, will become a staple of every leader's library, much like his earlier title, *Leading from the Second Chair*. Having known Mike now for over twenty years as leader of change, I can say with confidence that not only are the principles he shares accurate, but they flow from his experience of leading change so well in so many contexts. Whether you lead a church, a corporation, a nonprofit, a team, or your family, you need this book."

—GREG LIGON, president, Ligon Group

"I once saw a little comic in a magazine. The top read, 'Church plant week 2.' In the picture of people sitting in church, one man is leaning sideways to say to his wife, 'That's not how they did it *last* week.' The point is, change resistance happens in every organization regardless of how old or young it is. So, stewarding change is a part of every leader's job description. Mike totally gets this, and he's been leading churches and organizations through seasons of change for several decades. This book brings together what he's learned in all his experience, and it does so with his trademark 'boots on the ground' wisdom. The value here is the life and ministry experience found scattered throughout the pages of this book. It is money and time well spent."

—PHIL TAYLOR, coach, consultant,
author at Backstage Pastors

"Mike Bonem knows what he's talking about in ministry and in leadership. As anyone in a position of leadership knows, there are challenges. If you are a minister, you know it's not always easy. Leading as a minister can and will get messy. Fortunately, help is available and it's right here in Mike's new book. You'll be encouraged, motivated, and blessed as you read and apply the principles he shares."

—DAVID HARDAGE, executive director, Texas Baptists

"What an invaluable resource on leading change from someone with seasoned expertise to speak with authority on the subject. Mike Bonem has written a fabulous book with exceptionally helpful insights on the courageous artistry of leading people through ministry-related change, however messy it may be."

—LEO SCHUSTER, lead pastor, City Church Houston

The Art of Leading Change

Mike Bonem

The Art of Leading Change

Ten Perspectives on the Messiness of Ministry

Fortress Press
Minneapolis

THE ART OF LEADING CHANGE
Ten Perspectives on the Messiness of Ministry

Cover image: Easel, Katyrena Yakovlieva / shutterstock.com
Cover design: Brad Norr Design

Print ISBN: 978-1-5064-8506-5
eBook ISBN: 978-1-5064-8507-2

To our grandsons,

Theodore and William,

and the grandchildren we
have yet to meet.

May the church always be willing to
change so that you and future generations
experience the love and grace of Christ.

Contents

Contents

Introduction

One sentence has stuck with me for years: "We must continually choose between deep change or slow death."* This quote, from the introduction of Robert Quinn's *Deep Change*, describes the reality that I have seen in countless churches and ministries. We have a choice to make. And too many are consciously or unconsciously choosing slow death.

But we don't have to resign our churches, our ministries, and ourselves to the path of slow death. The choice may seem obvious, but the path of deep change is filled with hurdles. Most of those hurdles have names—like Paul or Julie or Tim. Leaders often believe that creating a better plan will ensure success, but it's the people, not the plans, that will determine whether a change gains traction. The purpose of this book is to explore the messiness of leading people through change. Because understanding these complex human and organizational dynamics will enable you to lead more effectively and move your church or ministry toward its God-given potential.

I have written and taught about leading change for over two decades. When speaking at conferences, my introduction often includes the statement "Leading change is both art and science." In the past I have focused on the science. After all, the "science" of change is easier to teach. The science is found in the strategies and priorities and processes that fill leadership books.

The *art* of leading change, on the other hand, is much more difficult to convey in a seminar. It can't be put into a formula or a tidy box. It is where leaders wrestle with questions such as "Are we

---

* Robert E. Quinn, *Deep Change: Discovering the Leader Within* (San Francisco: Jossey-Bass, 1996), xiii.

1

moving too fast or too slow?" "Do we have enough support to move forward?" "Should we attempt this bold, risky initiative, or is it better to take smaller steps right now?"

In each of these questions and dozens more that leaders ask on the transformational journey, the answer is unique to a particular context. In one case, boldness is the right answer, while in another, the same bold step would be pure folly. A rapid pace of change may seem reckless in a congregation in which the resistance is daunting, and the exact same pace may seem timid in a different congregation that is desperate for something new.

What is the primary distinction between the science and the art of leading change? People! The science of change leadership doesn't ignore the human element, but it tends to overlook the differences among people and the significant impact those differences have on how to best lead change. The art of leading change is all about people. We can't do the work God has called us to do without people, and yet each individual—and each collection of individuals—is unique. That's what makes leadership in a church so challenging.

The story of one change and two people illustrates this messy and unpredictable human element. The pastor and leadership team at West End Church* wanted to add a new worship service to attract younger families. As the tentative plans were shared with the congregation, several people raised concerns and questions. Jerry, a longtime member and leader among the senior adults, believed any style other than traditional was "less worshipful." Rachel, a former board chair and leader of the largest Bible study class, thought the change was a bad idea because it would "split the church." Both expressed their concerns privately to the pastor and publicly in group meetings.

After a period of listening to input, the board decided to proceed with the change. Rachel left West End and joined another church, but Jerry stayed. One Monday morning a few months after

---

* Fictional names are used for churches and individuals throughout this book, but the stories are all based on real examples.

the new worship service was launched, Jerry stopped by the pastor's office. He was smiling as he said, "I peeked into the sanctuary during the new worship service yesterday. I was amazed at the number of young families and how engaged they were in worship."

Jerry's story shows that people's minds and hearts can change, even when they appear to have dug in their heels. He might not have reversed course, however, if he had not felt loved by West End's pastor, who listened respectfully to his concerns. What about Rachel? She was treated with the same love and respect, but she chose to leave. As a former board chair, she was accustomed to swaying the outcome on major decisions and couldn't stomach being on the "losing" end this time. She thought most of her class would follow her out the door and was surprised when all but one family stayed at West End.

One story, two people, two very different individual outcomes. This is the uncertain human nature of leading change in churches and ministries. In the case of West End, Rachel's departure was disappointing, but the church barely missed a beat as the new worship service attracted many new families. Other stories don't have such positive outcomes. In a different church, the same scenario could play out with several key leaders following their "Rachel" out the door, effectively splitting the church and crippling its ability to implement a proposed change.

Leading congregational change is complex because it always involves people, and people are complex. Despite this complexity, leading change does not need to be based on uninformed guesses about how people might respond. Even the art of leading change involves science, but it's the science of people—especially the hows and whys that explain the reactions of people to change. These are the perspectives every leader needs to develop.

Leading *People* through Change

This book is a resource to help you better understand and practice the art of leading people through change. It's about harnessing people who are excited, swaying people who are reluctant, dealing with people who are resistant, and engaging people who are apathetic—all within the complexities of today's church and ministry settings. Deep organizational change is difficult, so you will not find simple answers in the pages that follow. But you will find perspectives and principles that serve as signs for the change journey. Some of the signs will be yellow cautions alerting you to pitfalls to avoid. Some will be green arrows pointing to paths with fewer obstacles. All the signs relate to people.

The heart of the book describes ten perspectives for the messiness of ministry. (I should add that ministry is always messy.) Each perspective underscores an important principle for leading change. They are not sequential, so you should feel free to skip around to the ones that speak to your current needs. Scattered between the ten perspectives are several "Artist's Perspectives," brief segments that offer fresh insights on leadership by looking through the lens of art.

The ten perspectives are bookended by two other essential concepts. The beginning examines "The Challenge of Change." Leading effectively requires understanding the contours and underlying reasons that make change difficult. Some of those contours are generic for any organization, but the most challenging ones are unique to churches and ministries.

The final chapter of the book explores "The Courage for Change." Because no matter how much you learn, leading change is difficult. Every change leader has scars to show for their efforts; some also have stories of victory to celebrate. Before any leader begins the change journey, they should ask if they have the courage and conviction to finish it.

Curious about the ten perspectives that make up the heart of the book? Here is a preview:

1   *Lead with Trust.* People simply won't follow a leader they don't trust. Building trust early in the journey is essential, and it pays big dividends later.

2 *Dig Beneath the Surface.* Culture is an invisible but powerful force that can impede change if leaders don't understand and address it.

3 *Take the Right Next Step.* People don't need to know every step of the change journey, but they want to know the overall vision and what to do next.

4 *Heavy Loads Require Strong Teams.* Choosing the right people to design and spearhead change should be a forethought, not an afterthought. Without them, it won't get off the ground.

5 *You Can't Please Everyone.* Pastors and ministry leaders have a deep desire to help people. But trying to keep everyone happy is a formula for gridlock and frustration.

6 *Resisters Are* Not *the Enemy.* It is tempting to ostracize the people who oppose a change, but they may have a valuable perspective to share and an important role to play.

7 *Momentum Is Your Friend.* Every successful experiment and small win, if used intentionally, can build enthusiasm and become a building block for future changes.

8 *What They Heard, Not What You Said.* Communication is an underpinning of every successful change process, but leaders often miss cues that they haven't been heard.

9 *Who Is* Not *in the Room?* Leadership teams need to shift their mindset, thinking less about their own needs and more about the outsiders who don't have a seat at the decision-making table.

10 *Look Up Before You Look Ahead.* For change efforts to produce congregational vitality, leaders must genuinely seek to follow God first.

I could have used more sterile, technical language to describe each of these perspectives. My hope is that these ten phrases will stick in your memory, at least subconsciously, so that they resurface as checkpoints in the change process. When someone pushes back on a new initiative, and you feel your blood pressure rising, you can remember that "resisters are not the enemy."

The perspectives are written as axioms that can create a common language for a staff or board* to learn and use together. Whether you read the book as a group or simply teach the concepts, these brief phrases can become a shorthand that guides decisions. Imagine your leadership team is discussing a significant programming change and someone wisely asks, "Who is not in the room that we should be thinking about?"

If you think this book is only for senior pastors and others in "first chair" roles, think again. It's for anyone who is on the front lines of leading change in a church or ministry. It's for executive pastors and other "second chair" leaders who stand shoulder to shoulder with the first chair, often as the chief implementers of change. It's for the volunteer board members who offer wise counsel and oversight for future-shaping decisions. And it's for those who are leading individual ministry areas, where the hard work of change occurs day by day and person by person.

Similarly, this book is not just for churches and ministries that were started many years ago. We may think of older congregations as being the most change resistant, but it doesn't take long for a new one to develop entrenched habits. "This is how we've always done it" is equally challenging whether "always" refers to three years or three decades.

Perspectives on the art of leading change are of little value if they're not put into practice. One Christmas, my sister's husband was given a video series by a well-known visual artist. My brother-in-law is not a professional, but he has a good eye and a natural artistic ability. The videos can't guarantee that he will become an expert, no matter how closely he studies them, but they can help him improve *if he practices*. Watching the videos is just the first step.

---

* *Board, elders,* and *leadership team* are used throughout this book as generic terms to represent the governance and decision-making bodies of churches and ministries.

The hard work, and the resulting growth, will occur when he picks up a paintbrush. Sure, he will make mistakes, but each mistake is an opportunity to learn and improve.

The same is true about studying the art of leading change. You may not become the next cover story in a church growth magazine, but learning and practicing the art will improve your proficiency. My goal is not just to give you a better *understanding* of the principles for leading people through change. I believe leadership can be learned, but the best learning occurs through *practice*. For this reason, each perspective concludes with specific questions and activities to help you apply what you have learned.

Leading *Yourself* to Change

Leading organizational change always requires personal change. Robert Quinn says when we "leave our comfort zone and step outside our normal roles . . . we learn the paradoxical lesson that we can change the world only by changing ourselves."*

On any personality assessment tool, I'm portrayed as being task-oriented more than people-oriented and valuing accomplishments more than relationships. I don't know how much of this is the result of nature versus nurture. But I'm certain that majoring in engineering as an undergraduate and later receiving an MBA reinforced whatever tendencies I already had. Simply stated, the science of leading change is naturally more comfortable for me than the art.

Even though I'm wired this way, I can't lead well staying in my comfort zone. Neither can you. For me, the journey of personal change has meant slowing down and listening more. It has pushed me to be more transparent about my emotions, more honest about my mistakes, and more accepting of missteps by others.

---

* Quinn, *Deep Change*, 9.

I don't know what comfort zone you may need to leave to lead well. But this is a book about personal change as much as it is about organizational change. So pay attention to the moments of discomfort as you dive into each perspective. Those may be gentle nudges from the Holy Spirit helping you see a place where change is needed within.

———————

This book was written in the middle of a global pandemic during which most churches and ministries were forced to make rapid, dramatic changes. Those changes were caused by external forces over which leaders had no control. As difficult as it was to make those adjustments, the changes beyond the pandemic will be far more difficult. That is when the pressure to "get back to normal" will collide with the opportunity to make significant shifts in ministry models. This pressure is not just a postpandemic phenomenon; it is the norm for leaders in a post-Christian society. We need new wineskins, but too many insiders are fighting to preserve the old ones. When tension around future direction is high, the art of leading change is an indispensable skill.

Leading people through change is never a straight line from A to B. There will always be unexpected twists and turns. But if you're interested in gaining a few navigation tools to lessen the heartache and improve the outcomes, I invite you to turn the page.

The Challenge of Change

I have good news and bad news. Which do you want to hear first? Whenever I'm presented with this question, my response is, "Let's get the bad news out of the way." I hope you agree, because this chapter contains the bad news: *change is difficult.*

You may be saying, "That isn't news." You already know that making any kind of meaningful change is difficult, personally or organizationally. At the individual level, think about an exercise program or diet that you tried to start. Or a relational reset that you attempted. It's not easy to break out of old habits and establish new patterns.

Organizational change takes the challenge of individual change and multiplies it across an entire group of people. When it's done well, you can harness the energy of a few people to change an entire organization—but now I'm jumping ahead to the good news. The negative side is that group dynamics often create a complex web that snares even well-designed change efforts.

So before we can dig into the good news that change is possible, we need to understand the bad news better. Why is change so difficult, especially when it's obvious that change is needed? And why does it seem to be especially difficult in church and ministry settings?

Go back to the challenge of making personal changes. One of the biggest obstacles is that the "cost" of making the change is high on the front end, and the benefits are generally less certain and further down the road. Starting an exercise program means sore muscles. If your plan involves a fitness class or some other group activity, another cost may be the embarrassment of appearing out of shape in front of friends or strangers. And the benefits? You hope you will feel better in a few months and will have better cardiac health in future years.

Personal changes also require an investment of time and energy on the front end. You may be convinced it would be good to learn a second language, but you know it will take hours and hours to become proficient. Those hours will need to be taken from some other activity, presumably something that you enjoy or believe to be important.

Expand from personal to organizational change and the same obstacles will exist, whether in a business or school or church. And the involvement of more people translates into additional barriers that change leaders must navigate. One of the biggest barriers to change in any organizational setting is a *desire for stability*. Most people want a certain degree of predictability in their lives. The bigger the change, the more instability and chaos they will experience. If they anticipate disruption on the horizon, they are likely to resist.

Have you noticed that younger people tend to be more open to change? *Past experiences* are one reason that resistance goes up with age. The longer we are alive, the more likely we are to have endured a promising change initiative that went awry. Bad memories from those past experiences will become the fuel for future resistance.

Even if change doesn't bring up bad memories from the past, it may represent a future *threat to power* for some people. The only reason to undertake significant organizational change is because of the expected benefits. But not everyone benefits equally. When people in the organization do the math of change and conclude they will lose, they push back. The "loss" may relate to influence, prestige, finances, employment, or other factors.

One of the most significant losses can be reputational damage if a proposed change *implies past mistakes*. People with long tenures in an organization, especially if they've been in leadership, often hear a proposal for change as an indictment of their past contributions. When blame is in the air, defensiveness and resistance are quick to follow.

The common denominator of these four barriers is *people*. None of the obstacles is due to bad ideas about the kind of change to make, even though that can certainly sink the effort. Even when an idea is brilliant, it's the people and their response to proposed changes that make the difference between success and failure.

This chapter started with the statement that change is difficult, but that is only the first part of the bad news. The second part is that change in churches and other ministry settings is more complicated and more difficult than in business. You may have sensed that intuitively, but do you know why?

The ministry of the apostle Paul provides a clue to this difficulty. In city after city, his proclamation of the good news of Jesus began in the synagogue. And in city after city, he found the message rejected by religious leaders who couldn't imagine making such sweeping changes in their lives and their religion. In each case, Paul walked away from the religious establishment, finding gentiles who were more open to the message and the change it entailed.

Paul's experience underscores the obstacles listed previously, but the roots of the challenge go even deeper in his story, and probably in yours as well. If you're going to lead a significant change effort in your church or ministry, you need to understand the unique, hidden barriers that stand in the way. The rest of this chapter shines a light to help you see them more clearly.

Untouchable Traditions

The Christian faith is rich in traditions and rituals. These traditions are deeply meaningful to the individuals who comprise each faith community. Some traditions are practiced across a broad spectrum of the church, such as a candlelight worship service on Christmas

Eve. Others are unique to a particular congregation, such as singing a particular song as a benediction each week.

If you're thinking that "traditions" are challenges only for old or mainline congregations, think again. Even a congregation that was started relatively recently or that isn't part of a denomination can quickly develop untouchable traditions. Any activity to which someone would say "That's just how we do things here" is a tradition. It can be the way that children are involved in worship just as easily as a specific communion liturgy.

A new pastor created an unintentional firestorm on his very first Sunday when he walked down the center aisle at the end of the worship service. It seemed like a simple and reasonable thing to do. He had been told that the congregation liked to greet their pastor at the door after the service. But the previous, long-tenured pastor always exited down the side aisle. The retired pastor frequently told the congregation that God should be the focus of their attention at the end of worship, and he didn't want to distract from that. The unfortunate new pastor hadn't been given that valuable nugget of information, which resulted in his violation of a "sacred" tradition.

In *Built to Last*, authors Jim Collins and Jerry Porras say that the most effective organizations "preserve the core and stimulate progress."* They explain that a well-defined core is essential and must be protected. But anything that is not at the core of an organization's identity can be changed if needed to build a thriving organization.

Most churches, if they heard this concept, would have difficulty identifying their "core" that must be preserved. If you leaned into this exercise by asking what must not be changed under any circumstances, the resulting list would be long and discouraging. Almost everything they do would be on their "must not change" list, leaving very little room to stimulate progress. The leadership team of a church rarely says this directly. In fact, they often say they're willing

---

* Jim Collins and Jerry I. Porras, *Built to Last: Successful Habits of Visionary Companies* (New York: HarperBusiness, 1997), 80.

to make whatever changes are necessary. But when a specific change is proposed, the challenge of traditions will be felt quickly.

Theological Overlay

Overcoming resistance anchored in traditions can be a challenge in any organization. But in churches, traditions are often infused with theological rationale that gives them even greater power. It's one thing to say "We've always done it this way" and quite another to say "The way we've always done it is God's way."

Sometimes the invocation of God's name is explicit. Often it is just implied. At times, people who want to preserve the status quo will point to a specific Bible passage to support their point of view. In other cases, they can't find the supporting verse but they're certain it exists. In all these situations, the theological overlay creates an additional obstacle to change.

Many churches celebrate the completion of high school with a "senior Sunday" for their students. There's no question that this is an opportunity to honor the work God has done in the students' lives and to encourage them to continue walking with God as they enter adulthood. But is it necessary to have this celebration on a Sunday morning? Does it need to be done the same way every year? Sure, that may be the tradition, but there are many ways to honor God as a church celebrates its seniors. Imagine suggesting that the event be moved to a Sunday night to allow more time to truly celebrate the seniors. The change conversation might suddenly take a theological turn when a group of parents objects that the celebration is becoming "just another secular event rather than the holy moment that occurs in the morning worship service."

Whenever a church or ministry is considering a significant change, the decision should be guided by prayer and by the Holy Spirit. This is true whether the final decision is to proceed with or pause a change. But remember that some of history's biggest opponents of change—the Pharisees—claimed to be obeying God even as they resisted the coming of the kingdom.

Dependence on Volunteers

Volunteers are the lifeblood of every church and most other ministries. By itself, that's a good thing. Think of how little we'd accomplish if all the work had to be done by paid staff. Can you imagine not having volunteers to teach Bible stories to children or to welcome visitors or to package and distribute food for people who need a meal?

Volunteers are essential, but reliance on them creates additional obstacles to leading change. A change initiative in business ultimately requires buy-in from employees. But business leaders have two extra tools to use: the power of the paycheck and the presence of the workforce.

If resistance arises, a business leader can resort to a top-down approach: "Make this change or else." The "or else" phrase is understood to mean a demotion or even termination of employment. This isn't the best tool to use, but it is available. In addition, the business workforce is on the job for 40 hours a week, which gives leaders ample opportunities to explain the whys and hows of a proposed change.

Compare this to a church. How many times has a member complained "I didn't know anything about that"? You know the information has been widely communicated, but you can't make meetings mandatory, and there are no real consequences for the member not reading their email. Even more challenging is that volunteers often feel free to do what they want, regardless of the new direction that is proposed. They may quit when asked to change. An even worse scenario is when they continue in their roles without making the requested changes.

A church decides to shift its emphasis from giving money for missions to engaging people in hands-on mission work. Their strategy is to mobilize people through the existing small groups and Bible study classes. So what should the pastor do if a small group leader decides not to participate? The leader might even tell the small group that the shift is a "stupid idea," thereby infecting others with the germ of resistance. When dealing with reluctant volunteers, especially ones who are long-tenured or dearly loved, the solution is never simple.

Multiple Motivations

Let's be honest. People are not always honest about their motivations. Sometimes they have not done enough soul-searching to even know their true motivations. And in Christian organizations where everyone knows how to give a "Sunday school answer," this can be confusing and can hinder change.

This sounds judgmental, but think about the most recent moment in your church when people were not on the same page about an important decision. There's a good chance that each leader would say they were advocating for a position based on prayer and following God's guidance. I doubt anyone would admit that their motivation was personal comfort or the happiness of a group of friends. And yet those more human and less spiritual motivations may be just below the surface.

The contemporary worship service at a church has grown steadily, but the 8:30 a.m. start time is seen as a deterrent to attracting first-time visitors. The pastor proposes changing the Sunday schedule, swapping the contemporary service and the 11:00 a.m. traditional service. Those objecting to the change say things like "Those young families are up early anyway." They also say "I don't sense God leading us to make this change." What you won't hear is "I like things the way they are" or "My spouse will be angry if I vote in favor of this change" or even "I don't really want to reach a lot of new, younger families." They may be harboring these thoughts, but they are rarely voiced.

When leaders are less than honest about their motivations, it becomes even more difficult to make decisions. We may wonder what they're really thinking, but no one wants to ask, "Did you truly pray about this? Are you confident that this is God's prompting and not just a personal preference?" And in truth, most leaders genuinely want to make decisions that are best for the church and in accordance with God's will. But that desire may be swept away in a flood of competing emotions and motivations.

Confusing Governance

A new pastor typically asks for a description of the church's governance structure. How many people are on the board? How are they selected? What committees exist and how much authority do they have? A seasoned pastor goes deeper, asking how decisions are really made. That's because what happens in practice may not resemble the official process.

In one church, the facilities committee has an outsized influence on strategic, board-level decisions. They have wielded this influence for so long that no one even questions it. When a new ministry initiative is being considered, board members say, "That's an interesting idea. Let's see if the facilities folks will support it."

This kind of confusion over governance and decision-making authority inhibits change in more than one way. The obvious problem is when change can be blocked by a shadow group that operates outside of the official process. But equally troubling is the way that this behavior discourages change champions and squelches the momentum for change.

Long Reach of History

The past is always present. This simple statement is one every leader should keep in mind. It often explains why one church is enthusiastic about trying new things and another seems to resist even the smallest change.

Organizations—churches in particular—have long memories. When a church has a history of successfully navigating change, people are more receptive to proposals for future shifts. "Success" in this context is multifaceted. It's not just about the overall outcome of a decision. People's recollections of success may include whether their voices were heard in the process, whether disagreements were handled in healthy ways, and whether they saw God at work in the changes. The negative side is equally powerful. A church's history with change might include a charismatic leader who was able to get a yes vote but didn't listen well. Or a proposed change that resulted in a small, vocal group angrily leaving the church. Or an expensive program that was "guaranteed to revive our church" that fell far short of its promises.

By all traditional measures, the launch of the church's first satellite campus had been an incredible success. A launch group of 50 people had grown to over 200 in worship attendance in less than 18 months. Offerings at the satellite were already covering its expenses. There was a buzz in the community about the new church. And yet when the opportunity arose to add a third campus, church leaders were surprisingly hesitant. In meetings, the verbalized concern was "We're not quite ready." In private, those leaders felt that the earlier campus decision had been pushed primarily by their pastor and had killed the momentum at the main campus.

History, as it relates to change, is tricky because it tends to be exposed in fragmented spurts. Pastors may try to understand the history at the start of their tenure, and they will typically learn a great deal. But they should never assume they know the entire backstory and the shadow it may cast over future decisions.

Lack of Meaningful Evaluation

The final factor that makes change more complicated in churches is the difficulty in evaluating results. Every business looks at the "bottom line," its profitability, as a measure of success. But churches often disagree on what their bottom line is. Attendance in worship and in small groups, the number of new members, and giving are important metrics, but leaders admit that these are incomplete indicators of fruitfulness. Their dissatisfaction, however, rarely becomes a springboard to create more meaningful metrics or to develop a deeper understanding of the factors driving their desired outcomes.

To be clear, I do not believe that the important work of a church can always be expressed in numbers. Our ultimate desire is for people to have a relationship with Jesus Christ and to continue to grow spiritually. Our expectation is that spiritual growth will be manifested in a variety of ways, only some of which are quantifiable or at least measurable.* I also know that a church's efforts are only part of this equation. The more important part is the work of the Holy Spirit, which we certainly cannot control.

Nevertheless, it is important to recognize that the absence of metrics undermines change efforts. Change will always be met with resistance, and one way to overcome that resistance is to paint the picture of the anticipated future results. The right metrics can make the picture clearer. If a church plans to partner with a local elementary school by providing tutors to improve reading scores, they could say, "Many kids at our partner school are not reading at grade level." But if they want to move more people to act, they will explain, "Over 150 kids at our partner school are at least two grade levels behind in their reading. We want to reduce that number to less than 50 in the next three years, but we can only do that if we have 100 people from our church who agree to serve as tutors."

The lack of meaningful measurement exacerbates a related problem: reluctance to give honest feedback. A culture of "niceness" permeates most churches. It prevents individual conversations about job performance and realistic evaluations of ministries. Not giving

---

* My book, *In Pursuit of Great and Godly Leadership* (San Francisco: Jossey-Bass, 2012), includes an entire chapter on "Do You Measure What Matters?"

negative feedback may seem to be Christlike behavior, in contrast to the "heartless" world of business. But a lack of honesty about shortcomings leads to poor stewardship of resources and deprives people of the opportunity to improve.

Without honest feedback, one of the major motivators for change will be missing. You've heard the expression "If it ain't broke, don't fix it." The lack of meaningful evaluation in churches begs the question, "If it is broken, how will we know?"

———————————

I began this chapter by saying, "Let's get the bad news out of the way." You already knew the difficulty of leading change, and this chapter confirmed it. Perhaps you gained some new insights into the specific factors that obstructed your past attempts to lead change. You may be discouraged by a greater awareness of the height of the mountain that you need to climb for your next change journey.

But remember that this book contains good news. Change is difficult, but it is not impossible. Leading healthy change cannot be boiled down to a simple recipe, but you can gain new perspectives and learn principles that will increase your effectiveness and lighten your load. Change leadership will always be an art, so let's take out a canvas and begin the first lesson.

PERSPECTIVES
FOR
LEADING PEOPLE
THROUGH
CHANGE

AN *Artist's* PERSPECTIVE

Art Is Messy

I met local artist David Maldonado for coffee one day because I wanted to get more insights as I worked on the manuscript for this book. As we sat and talked, I couldn't help noticing David's hands. It was an early morning meeting, so I don't think he had been in his studio that day, but I noticed several paint stains on his skin and some dried paint under his fingernails. My observation has nothing to do with David's personal hygiene and everything to do with the messiness of art . . . and the messiness of ministry leadership.

It's impossible for a painter to avoid getting paint on himself, or for a sculptor to walk away from a piece of marble without being covered in a fine layer of dust. Imagine how silly it would be for one of these artists to say, "I want to create a beautiful work of art, but I don't want to get dirty in the process." If you were an art instructor and your students expressed this attitude, you would probably laugh at them. Or you might get frustrated and ask them to leave your program!

It would also be ridiculous if I visited a site where David was painting a mural and found him wearing a suit. He knows the work is messy and he dresses accordingly. For some artists, that means keeping a drawer of "work clothes"—worn and stained shirts and pants bearing clear evidence that their owner is an artist. Other painters wear coveralls that catch many of the stray splashes of color. Some art projects merit more serious precautions, such as wearing goggles to protect the artist's eyes from paint or marble chips. Regardless of their specific choice of clothes and accessories, an artist does not ignore the inherent messiness of their work, nor will they shy away because they might ruin an article of clothing.

The work of leading change in churches and ministries is always messy. The leader whose goal is to not get "dirty" will not be able to lead at all. If you're called to lead, don't be surprised and don't run away when you encounter the messiness of conflict or skepticism. Put on your work clothes—the ones with the stains of past experience—and maybe even some protective gear and dive into the messy work that lies ahead.

PERSPECTIVE 1

Lead with Trust

You have probably heard quotable sayings about leaders and followers such as "He who thinks he leads, but has no followers, is just taking a walk."* It is true that you can't be a leader if people are not following. We could debate whether the leader should be in front, or alongside, or even in a less-than-visible role behind followers. You may even prefer a different word than *follower*. But the real shortcoming with this and similar sayings is they paint a picture of someone who has already become a leader. They don't explain what prompts people to follow in the first place.

The purpose of followers is not to stoke a leader's ego. ("Look how many people are following me.") Instead, followers form the critical mass to propel a change forward. A church may be full of faithful members, but members don't make change happen. Followers believe in the vision for change, and they demonstrate their belief by doing their part to turn the vision into reality. If followers are missing, it will become painfully obvious when the hard work of implementation begins.

But what prompts people to become committed followers who will support a major change? Belief in the vision is important and will be discussed in perspective 3. But if you want to turn members into followers, the prerequisite that is most important and most frequently overlooked is *trust*.

---

* John C. Maxwell, *The 21 Irrefutable Laws of Leadership: Follow Them and People Will Follow You* (Nashville: Thomas Nelson, 2007), 20.

What Is Leadership Trust?

In *Canoeing the Mountains*, Tod Bolsinger accurately describes change as a journey into uncharted territory. He then offers this simple but profound observation: "In uncharted territory, trust is as essential as the air we breathe. If trust is lost, the journey is over."[*]

Why is trust overlooked so often? Two reasons stand out. First, the nature of their vocation causes ministry leaders to believe they should be seen as trustworthy. After all, pastors answer to a higher authority. A prohibition against lying is one of the Ten Commandments. Ministry leaders often become indignant if someone suggests they can't be trusted.

The second reason is that trust is viewed as bimodal. You either trust someone or you don't. And since ministry leaders are clearly not in the same category as cheaters and habitual liars, the logical conclusion should be to trust them at all times and in all things. Right?

Only it is not this simple. Trust is expressed in many forms and at many levels. My wife might trust me to pick up something from the grocery store, which only speaks to my dependability or memory. If I give a friend a $20 bill to get a latte for me when they go out for coffee, I trust them to bring back change. But would I trust the same person with a much larger sum of money?

These examples are the ground floor of trust. They are focused on ability (the knowledge and skills to do something), dependability, and accurately representing facts. While these attributes are important, no leader will succeed solely with this level of trust.

When our kids were young, our church's youth group had a great group of teens. We liked all of them and would trust any of them with simple tasks. But only a few were trusted enough to babysit our children. They repeatedly demonstrated that the things on earth we

---

[*] Tod Bolsinger, *Canoeing the Mountains: Christian Leadership in Uncharted Territory* (Downers Grove, IL: InterVarsity, 2015), 66.

treasured most—our children—were safe in their care. They loved our children and would have put themselves in harm's way to protect our kids.

Effective ministry leaders achieve this higher level of trust. It's the kind of trust where a follower is willing to take a risk or make a sacrifice, like standing firm when fellow church members oppose a new initiative. This is not the blind trust that we sometimes see with highly charismatic leaders. Rather, it is the hard-won trust that grows out of the accumulation of the everyday moments of leadership.

After three years as pastor of Highpoint Church, Ryan and the leadership team were frustrated by the lack of fruit in their discipleship ministry. Too many of the small groups existed primarily as social clubs rather than places that spurred spiritual growth. Newcomers to the church had difficulty breaking into groups because the relationships were so tight. Ryan had tried to nudge the groups toward different patterns, but his efforts had been unsuccessful. So as planning began for the new ministry year, Ryan and the leadership team were considering a proposal to revamp discipleship completely by eliminating most of the existing groups and starting new ones with a fresh mix of participants and a different meeting format.

No one on Highpoint's leadership team questioned the need for a change in their discipleship strategy. But as they continued to discuss the proposed revamp, the questions on everyone's minds were, Will this work? Will our small group leaders support it? Then one of the leaders said, "Ryan, you've been a breath of fresh air after all we went through with our last pastor. Everyone loves you and is glad you're here. But this is a big change. The real question is whether they trust you and the rest of us enough to make the sacrifices that will be required."

Sometimes leaders walk into an environment in which high levels of trust are bestowed upon them. Sometimes they start at rock bottom through no fault of their own. You have no control over how much trust you inherit, but you can shape the trajectory of trust. Your words and actions—big and small—can expand trust or erode it. Before examining how to build this kind of deeper trust, let's take a closer look at why it is lacking.

Why Is Trust Lacking?

"This is a great church. The people love God and are ready for the next pastor to lead them into the future." Countless new pastors have heard statements like this. And countless pastors have been frustrated in their first few months by the amount of resistance they encounter when they try to lead.

One of the reasons for this resistance has nothing to do with the current pastor and has everything to do with prior pastors. If "the past is always present," then previous breaches of trust will live for many years in a congregation's memory.

Trust can be broken in many different ways. Some are obvious, including moral failures or outright lying to the congregation. Before Ryan arrived as pastor, Highpoint had been in a virtual free fall. The previous pastor was forced to leave after an affair with a church member, and a two-year interim period followed. Attendance and giving had declined dramatically during that time, and the discipleship ministry had been largely ignored. When Ryan arrived, he knew that reestablishing trust, rather than a quick-fix program, was what the church most needed.

Major trust-busting moments like the earlier one at Highpoint make the headlines, but the losses of trust that are less glaring and more common can be just as damaging. Examples might include a pastor who says she hopes to spend the rest of her career at the church and then leaves after just three years. It may be a hiring process that seemed skewed to favor a personal acquaintance. It may happen when a leader verbalizes a commitment to support a new mission partnership but doesn't follow through.

These seem like small examples. In fact, pastors in cases like these may have had good intentions. The call to serve another church may have come out of nowhere. A leader may have believed that adding the mission partnership into the budget was sufficient "support." But perceptions are reality, and if the congregation *perceives* that a previous pastor was not trustworthy, the memory lingers far longer than the incident. When a new pastor arrives, those past experiences directly shape how much trust they inherit.

At a minimum, new ministry leaders need to understand the history of their organizations. As you construct the timeline and understand the key events, look for the evidence of effective or ineffective leadership. Listen for indicators that previous leaders were or were not trusted. Pay particular attention to stories that are filled with negative emotions such as sadness, anger, or bitterness. In what ways were past leaders perceived as not being trustworthy?

Of course, this is not just a lesson for new leaders who are trying to understand their predecessors. You may have been the one who eroded trust by not supporting the mission partnership or by pushing to hire a friend rather than another qualified candidate. You may think, "That was long ago, and I admitted to the board that I should have handled it differently." While admitting mistakes is an important step, it doesn't erase the memory.

Understanding the history of a church or ministry can help you understand the contours in which you are leading. Reflecting on your own leadership tendencies may highlight small ways that you are eroding trust. Do you avoid conflict and seem to agree with whoever you are talking to, or is your message consistent? Do you seem to exaggerate the positives and downplay any concerns, or do you give a balanced assessment? If a new initiative is ultimately unsuccessful, do you take ownership for the "failure"? And if it is successful, do you generously share the credit with the whole team, or do you appear to enjoy the spotlight a little too much? Each of these questions points to small instances when trust is either strengthened or weakened.

The erosion of earthen dams is one of the national infrastructure concerns that has become more prominent in recent years. These dams have been mostly ignored in the 50 or more years since their construction. They are much less noticeable than their larger concrete counterparts that form large lakes and provide electricity for entire cities. And yet the failure of a "small" earthen dam can be spectacular and catastrophic. While the failure happens in a flash, the erosion that leads to a failure occurs slowly and almost invisibly over many years.

In the same way, most of the problems with leadership trust are the results of slow erosion over time. The evidence of trust erosion may be sudden and dramatic—a disappointing capital campaign, a split vote on a major decision, low response to a church-wide initiative—but the underlying causes are like the many small drips that weaken that earthen dam.

How Is Trust Built?

Unlike the natural forces that cause physical erosion, the erosion of trust is not inevitable, unstoppable, or irreversible. Pastors and ministry leaders can and should be ever mindful of the ways in which they can build trust. How is this done?

Let's start by naming two common misconceptions about building trust. It does not happen by standing in front of a crowd and announcing, "You can trust me!" No matter how passionate or sincere you may be, public pronouncements do not increase trust. Nor is outward success the basis for building trust. Professional competence is important, but people have been disappointed too many times by leaders who had great track records and deceitful hearts.

Instead of big, flashy moments, trust is built on a foundation of *relationships*, *consistency*, and *integrity*. We may talk about whether a church trusts its pastor, but that is misleading. The real question is whether the *people* of the church trust their pastor. And the people want to know: Does the pastor genuinely care about me? Does she really mean what she said? Does his walk match his talk? When enough individuals answer yes to these questions, it coalesces into a collective expression of trust.

Relationships matter. The old adage is true: people don't care how much you know until they know how much you care. People are simply more likely to trust a leader who cares about them. The care must be genuine; if they sense an ulterior motive, the opportunity to build trust goes out the window. Even if you may feel an urgency to make something happen quickly, you still need to make the time to develop relationships. In the long run, these relationships can make the difference in the success or failure of a change initiative.

A few weeks after Ryan arrived at Highpoint, he shared an insight with his wife: "Before we got here, I thought I knew what this church needed. I had three different ministry priorities that I was convinced would turn things around. But I've realized none of those ideas are what they need right now. There is only one priority— loving the people by listening to their stories and caring for the hurt they've experienced the last few years." So that is what Ryan did for much of his first two years. This period of building relationships stabilized the church. But more importantly, it built a strong foundation of trust that paved the way for the leadership team to consider significant changes like the discipleship revamp.

The importance of relationships may be obvious, but the challenge with *consistency* is more subtle. Many leaders don't realize the impact of their words. They may not think anything of declaring, "Missions is our number-one priority" one day and the next day emphasizing, "We have to focus on discipleship." They may not even remember having told one person that this is the year to hold the line on spending, so they readily support someone else's request to increase the budget for youth. The leader may not think about this, but church members do. And these small inconsistencies can quickly erode trust. Trusted leaders are always mindful of what comes out of their mouths.

Early in his career, Ryan had been an associate pastor at a church where the senior pastor had a deep aversion to disappointing anyone in the congregation. As a result, the senior pastor tended to agree with whatever church member he was talking to in the moment, a practice that eroded their confidence in his leadership. At Highpoint, Ryan often prefaced his ideas by saying, "This is just a brainstorm. I'm not ready for us to act on it yet." In the same way, he gladly listened to proposals from church members, but he was careful to only make commitments he could keep.

A leader's words may be consistent, but *integrity* requires the leader's actions and words to match. Unfortunately, the broader society has learned that many leaders and public figures fall short of this standard. Politicians, business executives, and ministry leaders have frequently been caught doing the very things that they have insisted should not be done by their followers. Because this happens so often, the public has little tolerance for excuses, even in cases where the explanation is legitimate. It may not seem fair to be held to such a high standard, but pastors who want to build trust pay careful attention to the optics of their actions.

As Ryan prepared to talk to the leadership team about the discipleship revamp at Highpoint, he also prepared himself for the personal cost. The small group Ryan and his wife were in had been a life-giving refuge during their first three years, and the members had become some of their closest friends. He wanted to keep his group intact, but he knew he would lose credibility and undermine the revamp process if he did that.

The common thread that connects the trust building of relationships, consistency, and integrity is time. None of these happens overnight. All require the leader to take a long-term perspective. If you're stepping into a new role in a healthy church or ministry, plan on at least six months of intentional work to build trust. In a complex organization, or one where trust is low because of past issues, trust building will take at least a year and probably longer. And in either case, leaders should remember that the hard work of maintaining trust never ends.

Do They Actually Trust You?

This chapter started with the question "What prompts people to follow a leader?" While many factors come into play, trust is the essential prerequisite. But how do you know whether people actually trust you? It isn't helpful to find out after a vote is taken. And if ministry leaders ask directly whether people trust them, they rarely get an honest answer. Is it possible to get an early read on the level of trust a congregation has toward its leaders?

For major decisions, one way is to test the water early with key constituents. Capital campaigns often do a precampaign survey and ask for preliminary commitments. This practice is designed to avoid a disastrous culmination on "pledge Sunday." The underlying principle should not be limited to campaigns. Before going public with a discipleship revamp, Ryan and the leadership team can share the proposal with the church's existing small group leaders and then invite their feedback. Some people may question the rationale for the change. Others will focus on the mechanics of how it will be done. Still others may reflect the emotion associated with such a significant change.

Underneath these responses, Ryan and the leadership team should also listen for indicators of trust. Questions about their motives for making the change or any kind of accusation (e.g., "you've just been waiting for an opportunity to change all our groups") are clear signs of a trust deficit. If this happens, the likelihood of a successful change effort is close to zero. On the other hand, if trust is high, many of the leaders will get on board despite their concerns. Even those who don't are less likely to create obstacles.

A more important and widely applicable way to assess trust is to create a culture where honest feedback is the norm. The familiar fable of the "emperor's new clothes" is an example of the opposite culture. In the fable, fear prevents the people from telling the emperor that his "invisible" garments have left him exposed (literally!). Replace the word *fear* with *niceness* and you have a description of the culture of many ministries. People don't tell the truth because the truth would hurt the leader's feelings, and that wouldn't be "nice."

A culture of niceness won't change instantly, but pastors can move the needle by asking for meaningful feedback. Feedback shouldn't be limited to issues directly related to trust. It can and should include all aspects of organizational and leadership effectiveness: clarity of vision, development of other leaders, the success of a strategic initiative, and more. The more comfortable people are with giving feedback in general, the more likely they will be to share concerns about behaviors that erode trust.

When it comes to feedback on trust, broad questions will rarely yield helpful answers. Asking "Do you trust me?" implies that there are only two options and will almost always result in a yes answer. It's better to ask questions that are more specific to the issue at hand: Does the congregation trust us enough to move forward with this programming change? Have I done or said anything in the last month that has eroded the congregation's trust in me?

Even these questions might be difficult to answer with a larger group such as a board or leadership team. The best assessment of trust occurs when a leader has the right close advisors. If you want to know the truth, pick a small handful of people whom you trust, who care deeply about you *and* the church, and who have a reputation for being honest, even a little blunt. Explain to them that leading with trust is the only way that the church or ministry will be able to reach its God-given potential. Acknowledge that you, like every leader, have blind spots. And tell them that one of the greatest gifts they can give you and the church is to provide you with honest feedback, especially if you do something that damages trust.

It may feel scary or risky to invite this kind of honest feedback. Hearing the ways that your words or actions have eroded trust can be difficult. But it is even riskier to lead without knowing, and even more damaging to find out that trust is lacking after a major change has been launched.

Will Ryan and the leadership team be successful in revamping discipleship at Highpoint? The answer is uncertain. There are no guarantees in this or any other significant change effort. It is clear, however, that Ryan has taken a number of important steps to build trust. And if I need to predict which leaders will or won't succeed when major shifts are being made, I'll always pick the ones who have laid a strong foundation of trust.

FROM PERSPECTIVE TO PRACTICE

LEAD WITH TRUST

- Create a timeline of your church or ministry with the names of previous leaders and major decisions and events. Invite other leaders to contribute to this effort. What themes do you see? What can you learn from the past that informs your understanding of trust in the present?
- Identify a small group of people whom you can trust to give you feedback. Explain to them the importance of trust and your hope that they will give you honest observations about your leadership, especially any moments when trust is eroded.
- Think about a proposal that failed due to insufficient support or where you struggled to get enough buy-in. Assess the reasons for the lack of support. What role did trust play?
- Relationships, consistency, and integrity are the key building blocks of trust. Self-evaluate how you are doing with each of these. Ask your trusted advisors for their evaluations.

PERSPECTIVE 2
Dig Beneath the Surface

If *trust* is essential as a foundation for individual change leaders, what is its organizational equivalent, the powerful force that is often taken for granted? It's organizational culture, which can be a building block or a stumbling block for meaningful change. And just like trust, the importance of culture is often ignored because it exists primarily at an unconscious level, beneath the surface of the church or ministry's decisions, processes, and programs.

Every church or ministry has a culture that has been created over time by hundreds of events. Even a brand-new congregation quickly develops its own culture. Ask someone to describe their church, and if they answer honestly, you'll gain insights into the culture. "We are ____." Risk-takers or cautious. Friendly or cliquish. Comfortable or hungry. Fast-moving or deliberate. Trusting or skeptical. Agreeable or contentious. These attributes are the hidden but powerful threads that together make the fabric of organizational culture.

Threads and fabric provide a helpful way to think about culture. You may like a particular fabric that is colorful or breathable or feels good. You may dislike a fabric that is bland or rough. But your opinion is actually based on the blending of thousands of threads that make the fabric. Burlap is scratchy because of the threads that are used to make it. In the same way, a single word isn't enough to describe the richness and complexity of a church's culture.

The fabric analogy is helpful, but it is also inadequate on an important point. Once the threads are woven together, the fabric cannot be changed. Is culture the same? After the first couple of years, is an organization's culture locked in place forever? The good news is that culture change is possible. The bad news is that culture change takes time and hard work.

While changing a culture is not easy, it is often the precursor to the more visible, strategic changes that a leader hopes to accomplish. A popular saying, often attributed to leadership guru Peter Drucker, highlights this point: "Culture eats strategy for breakfast." Leaders often spend hours developing strategy and the initiatives to support the strategy. That's understandable; strategy is more tangible and exciting. Organizational culture is squishy and harder to get your hands on. But if you ignore the underlying culture, your strategic planning will be in vain. Effective change leadership is always a culture-shaping endeavor.

Understanding the Culture

Paul was one of the newest members of St. John's Church, but the pastor and several other leaders had already taken note of his involvement. He regularly participated in worship and a small group, contributed to the budget every month, volunteered with one of their mission partners, and was enthusiastic about the vision. He seemed like an ideal member, someone who could step into a leadership role.

Then one week as his small group meeting ended, Paul commented on the recently announced decision to cancel the Saturday night worship service: "I know they said it was 'a prayerful decision' made by the board, but it sounds like Pastor Alison duped the others into rubber-stamping the decision because she was tired of working on Saturdays." The small group leader was taken aback at first. Then he pulled Paul aside. "It sounds like you have a real concern about the decision, Paul. But that's not how we do things here."

Paul furrowed his brow, and the anger in his voice was obvious as he spoke: "What do you mean? Does everyone here just blindly follow Alison?" The small group leader calmly replied, "That's not what I'm saying. But in this church, if someone has a concern with a decision, they go directly to the decision-makers. We believe that's the biblical model. Anything else is unhealthy or even divisive."

We'll explore resistance in depth in perspective 6. For this chapter, the key phrase in the story is "that's not how we do things here." When a behavior or decision or process is explained with "that's not how we do things" or "that's just how we do things," the threads in the fabric of culture are being revealed.

Paul's story illustrates two important threads of the culture at St. John's. One relates to decision-making. Alison and the board are responsible for making major decisions. The church does not have an autocratic culture where the pastor acts unilaterally, nor is it one where the congregation is formally involved in every consequential decision.

The second, less visible cultural element in the story relates to disagreement and conflict. What happens when a member doesn't like a decision or has some other concern with a leader in the church? In some congregations, gossip and triangulation are the norm. The pattern of behavior, which is never named but easily observed, is to "talk to anyone other than the person you're upset with, especially if you think you'll get a sympathetic ear." In other congregations, dissent is quickly squelched by the core leaders, and dissenters are ostracized. St. John's seems to have a different culture, one that allows for disagreement but expects it to be handled in a biblical and respectful way.

Pause for a minute and start a list of "how we do things" in your church or ministry. As you make your list, try to identify the behaviors and habits that happen almost automatically, that insiders do without thinking twice. What would an attentive outsider observe?

Like Paul, you may have been conditioned to accept a culture where triangulation and passive aggressive behavior are the norm. When you read the earlier vignette, you may have wondered, "What's going on in this church to prompt a small group leader to say, 'That's not how we do things here'?" Whether you realize it or not, your curiosity is about the underlying culture.

Your list of cultural elements should not be limited to making decisions and dealing with conflict. Your list may include how finances are handled or where the real power resides. For example, a church may have a well-defined process for making decisions, but two wealthy members are able to reverse those decisions in quiet, offline meetings with the board chair. Cultural threads include the way guests are treated, the ease of launching new ministries, or the church's external reputation. A church that rapidly mobilizes to serve people in moments of crisis because "it's what we do" is another example of culture at work.

A Deeper Understanding

Identifying the important threads of organizational culture is a helpful step, but the real power comes from understanding why. If culture is "just how we do things," wise leaders ask, "Why do we do it that way?" They aren't satisfied with "Just because" or "I don't know" as the answer. The power to change culture comes with understanding the "why" behind it, which is often found in one or two pivotal events in the past.

Alison, the pastor at Paul's church, had been burned by unhealthy conflict in a prior pastoral experience. When she arrived at St. John's, she began to hear stories of the conflicts that led their previous pastor to resign. But leaders and church members all seemed eager to put this behind them, and they repeatedly asked Alison for her vision. The board assumed that their pastor's vision would be the focus for their annual retreat during her first year. So they were surprised when Alison explained, "I don't have a 'vision' for how big we will be in five years, or who we will be reaching, or how many worship services we will have. But I do have a vision that, regardless of how big or small we are, we will be healthy. And one of the best signs of health is how we treat each other, especially when we disagree."

The rest of the retreat was spent unearthing some of the past conflicts at St. John's and discussing what needed to change. They examined biblical passages on conflict (Matt 18), on unity in the body (John 17), and on humility (Phil 2). St. John's didn't change overnight—culture never changes quickly—but board members look back to the retreat as a turning point. If you ask, "Why is conflict handled so differently here than in most churches?" they will say it started at the retreat with Alison's bold challenge to follow biblical teachings.

"Why?" It's one of the most powerful words in a leader's vocabulary. It can lead to discovering deeper insights into the church and its culture. But the question isn't just for you. The same discussion of "why we do what we do" often uncovers hidden assumptions or past experiences that even long-tenured leaders have forgotten. Only after invisible beliefs have surfaced can a leadership team have a meaningful discussion about how their underlying assumptions might need to change.

Take the example of the church where two wealthy individuals have a history of reversing or revising decisions made by the governing board. The backstory is that their substantial gifts bailed the church out of a desperate financial crisis more than twenty years earlier. The unspoken belief is that a similar need could arise in the future, so it's important to keep these individuals happy by bending to their will.

What would happen if the current governing board unpacked this story and its associated assumptions? They might reach any number of conclusions: the pattern of reversing decisions is unhealthy, their fears show a lack of faith in God's ability to provide, or even the wealthy members aren't trying to be manipulative. Once these past incidents and the underlying assumptions are brought to light, leaders can establish different beliefs that will lead to different behaviors. It all starts with asking "Why?"

The familiar story of Jonah shows the importance and power of digging deeper to understand "why." If you read the opening of the story ("Jonah ran away from the Lord") for the first time, you might speculate on why Jonah is running away. You might reasonably assume that Jonah is afraid to preach to the wicked people of Nineveh and that he doesn't trust God to protect him. Or perhaps, like Moses at the burning bush (Exod 3), Jonah doesn't see himself as a great orator. The deeper reason for Jonah's flight isn't revealed until long after his encounter with the great fish. When Nineveh repents and the Lord relents, Jonah sulks. Why? He fled because he knew God's character and didn't want any part in a story in which Nineveh might repent and be spared: "I knew that you are a gracious and compassionate God, slow to anger and abounding in love, a God who relents from sending calamity" (Jonah 4:1–2).

Imagine being Jonah's companion but not knowing the real reason for his attempted escape. You might begin by simply emphasizing the importance of obeying a direct command from God. You might point out that even Tarshish is not beyond God's reach. You could follow your assumptions and reassure Jonah that God would give him the right words to say and would protect him from harm at the hands of the Ninevites. Would all these eloquent arguments change Jonah's behavior? No. Because they wouldn't address his actual concern.

As the story ends, God speaks to the real issue that is troubling Jonah: his belief that the people of Nineveh deserve God's punishment, not forgiveness. Jonah's attitude is understandable. Assyria, with its capital of Nineveh, was Israel's sworn enemy, the conquering nation that had plundered the Northern Kingdom, killed many of its people, and taken others captive. Jonah was simply a product of the culture in which he had lived his entire life. Animosity and hatred toward one's enemies were considered normal.

The final verses are God's appeal for Jonah to consider a different viewpoint, one that is open to the possibility of repentance and forgiveness for all people. Scripture doesn't record Jonah's reply, so we're left to wonder what he might have said. Perhaps it's good that the story is unresolved. It wouldn't seem realistic if Jonah simply replied, "You're right, Lord. Of course, the people of Nineveh deserve your love and forgiveness." While anything is possible with God, culture change rarely happens quickly.

Moving the Needle

So how does culture change occur? How can you begin to move the needle to create a culture that facilitates your church or ministry's vision? It takes steady, committed, persistent effort. It requires attention to formal processes and informal behaviors.

The culture change at St. John's Church illustrates this journey. What happened in the three years between the governing board's retreat and a small group leader telling Paul, "That's not how we do things here"? When the board members left the retreat, they had a new appreciation for what Scripture teaches about handling conflict and disagreement. They were more aware of past incidents when they and the congregation had fallen short of this standard. They expressed a unified commitment to act differently in the future.

But old patterns of behavior, anchored in an entrenched culture, don't shift rapidly. When one church member was unhappy with a poorly organized youth event, she shared her frustration with her friend Natalie, who was on the board. Rather than redirecting this person to talk to the youth director, Natalie responded, "I'll bring it up at our next meeting."

Alison's highest priority was for the church to become more unified and to learn to deal with disagreement because she knew this would pave the way for future changes. When Natalie expressed the concern about the youth event, Alison calmly stated, "I'll be glad for us to talk about the event and the youth director's performance, but let's talk about something else first. I wonder if this moment is an opportunity for us to revisit our conversation about biblical conflict resolution." She reminded the group of their commitments and led them in a discussion of different ways the specific situation could have been handled. At first, Natalie was defensive about her behavior. Wasn't it her responsibility as a board member to listen to concerns from church members and bring them to the board? But the gentle and nonjudgmental tone of the conversation helped her step back and gain a fresh perspective. By the end, Natalie agreed to go back and ask her friend to talk to the youth director as a first step.

Of course, this wasn't the only time board members slipped back into old ways of acting. A few months later, the board had a sharp disagreement about the budget for the coming year. After the meeting, Alison saw three people talking in the parking lot. As she walked over to join them, she heard one person describe the treasurer's proposal as "stupid and irresponsible." After a long day and a difficult meeting, Alison was tempted to ignore the remark, walk to her car, and drive home. Instead, she jumped into the conversation and, after listening for a minute, encouraged the frustrated board member to meet with the treasurer before the next meeting.

These incidents illustrate a key principle: the best way to move the cultural needle is to start in the center. The core leaders need to understand and agree with the desired shift in culture, and they need to support the change with their actions. It is far easier to sow the seeds for culture change, and for the resulting behaviors, with a small, committed group of leaders than with an entire congregation.

These stories also highlight the importance of accountability. Culture change is usually two steps forward and one step back. But in the absence of accountability, a single step back—when someone reverts to old patterns of behavior—will become multiple steps. Alison could have disregarded both situations as minor slips, but by gently holding the individuals accountable, she helped the entire board take another step forward toward their desired culture.

Culture change needs to start with the core leaders, but it can't stop there. The inner circle needs to be the catalyst for more widespread culture change. After several months, it became clear that the board members were living into the practices of healthy conflict resolution. So Alison started asking about their behavior outside of board meetings: "How have you demonstrated and encouraged unity in the body since our last meeting? Have you had any missteps that you need to make right?" She knew that having board members model the desired behavior would have a great influence on the congregation.

For unity and healthy conflict to be a priority, Alison also knew that she had to be the primary communicator. In her preaching, she often talked about the Bible's "one another" instructions, such as "love one another" (John 13:34 and other verses), "forgive one another" (Col 3:13), and "live in harmony with one another" (Rom 12:16). In leadership meetings, she often said, "If people can't see that our faith makes a difference in the ways we treat each other, they won't be interested in faith at all." She modified the new member class to include teaching on biblical ways to resolve disagreements.

If this sounds like a slow process and a lot of work, that's because it is. The culture of any church or ministry is like a rubber band (or multiple rubber bands). One end of the rubber band is attached to the assumptions and past experiences that shape current beliefs and behaviors. A leader may successfully do something different once or on a small scale, like intervening in a specific disagreement to model healthier practices. But the rubber band of culture wants to snap back to the old patterns.

Moving too quickly and aggressively to change a culture is like stretching a rubber band to its breaking point. It might look like the grip of old behaviors is broken, but it's more likely the rubber band will break, hurting the leader in the process. When significant culture change is needed, wise leaders play the long game. They know that continued stretching will eventually loosen the rubber band. They stay focused on one or a handful of elements of culture that need to change. They refrain from jumping to a new challenge until they see evidence that the desired culture is taking root.

Moving the needle of culture also requires a leader to withstand the pressure for immediate, visible results. The pressure for results may be created by a board, by general organizational expectations, or by a leader's internal wiring. Remember that the board at St. John's came into that first retreat hoping to hear an exciting vision from Alison. As she prepared for the retreat, she wondered how the board would respond to her emphasis on unity and health. Would they be supportive, or would they think, "Is that all she has for us?"

The pressure to deliver swift results rather than deep culture change rarely passes quickly. Typical measures of success seldom improve in the early stages of shifting culture. In fact, they may get worse. Alison's attempt at gentle accountability could have resulted in Natalie leaving the church and taking others along. If that had happened, attendance for the year would have declined. But isn't it better to have a slightly smaller congregation that is poised for healthy growth than to build on an unhealthy culture?

Ultimately, Alison's prayerful conviction led her to stick to her planned emphasis on changing the culture. This is not to say that everything else was put on hold at St. John's. Alison and the leadership team made several small changes and launched one new ministry during her second year. But as they continued to plan and make programming decisions, Alison was always mindful to not lose sight of her main priority.

The St. John's story focuses on shifting a church's culture toward healthier ways of dealing with disagreement and conflict. But that is just one example. What aspect of your church's culture most needs to change? It may be slow decision-making or a paralyzing fear of failure or extreme caution with finances. Maybe it's a posture of "me first" rather than "others first." Just remember that it is virtually impossible to implement meaningful change without first addressing the underlying beliefs and assumptions that stand in the way.

Is shifting a culture hard work? Yes. Messy? Without a doubt. Slow and sometimes painful? Unfortunately. And yet what would it be worth to have a church or ministry full of leaders who fully and deeply embrace the desired culture? How much stronger would your church be if, when a "Paul" behaved contrary to the culture, you could count on the leaders to gently but firmly respond, "That's not how we do things here."

FROM PERSPECTIVE TO PRACTICE

DIG BENEATH THE SURFACE

- What words describe your church or ministry's culture? Make your own list and invite your leadership team to do the same. Then compare your answers.
- Go deeper. Invite the leadership team to discuss the underlying "whys" that have created the most significant "threads" of the current culture.
- What biblical principles are most important for defining and shaping the desired culture?
- What is one element of culture that you and the leadership team would like to change? What is a first step you can take? Where will you encounter resistance?

AN *Artist's* PERSPECTIVE

The Purpose Behind the Art

In my conversation with local artist David Maldonado, one comment took me by surprise: "I don't enjoy painting. I enjoy what pushing paint *does*. I get to tell stories and build community." David is clear that his motivation is the bigger purpose for his art, just as a bigger purpose should motivate every leader.

David's visual art is expressed in a variety of ways, but two specific forms capture his desire to tell stories and build community. His commissioned murals are always a narrative without words. One of them can be found in a historically blue-collar area that was closely connected to the Port of Houston. As the neighborhood becomes gentrified, David's mural reminds the newer residents of a history they don't know. Another mural is being created to represent the theme of "Revive" for a city that wants to inspire its citizens with the vision of a vibrant future.

One of David's most interesting endeavors is "creative nights," when people in the community can come to his studio for a free night of music and art. Members of the audience are invited to collaborate on a piece of art by coloring one section of a sketch that David has started. The process draws out the creativity of the participants and builds an instant sense of community.[*]

---

[*] More information about David Maldonado's "creative nights" can be found at www.pandulcehtx.org.

Perhaps David's dislike of the work of "pushing paint" shouldn't have surprised me. I can't say that I enjoy writing. The ideation phase is energizing, but the tedious process of putting ideas into words and then editing (and reediting) to get the words right is how the bulk of my time is spent. It isn't fun. But just like David, my writing has a broader purpose that is deeply satisfying. When my words help leaders develop new skills and perspectives, and God breathes new life into their churches and ministries, it makes all the effort worthwhile.

I hope there are many aspects of leadership that you genuinely enjoy. I know the work of leading change in a church or ministry is hard and exhausting, and parts of it are truly unenjoyable. But you are not leading just for the sake of leading. Your role, as much as any other profession, has a great purpose behind it. In those moments when you wonder why you keep pushing paint or people, remember the greater purpose to which you have been called and for which you are leading.

Take the Right Next Step

When planning the next big initiative for your church, do you approach it like a NASA engineer preparing for a moon shot? Or are you more like one of the explorers of the sixteenth or seventeenth century?

NASA mission planners spend untold hours and countless dollars to anticipate everything that could go wrong and to eliminate all uncertainty and risk. Even though their failures have been dramatic and tragic, the truth is that they have been incredibly successful at putting people on the moon, landing spacecraft on Mars, and exploring the universe. NASA will not take the first step until every step has been planned in detail.

Contrast that with the explorers who couldn't possibly plan every step in detail. They couldn't consult the maps because they were the ones making them. They didn't know exactly what supplies to bring because they didn't know what they'd encounter. But they did have a compelling goal—reaching one of the poles, sailing around the globe, finding a better route—and they sought to achieve it. Sometimes they succeeded and other times they failed, but every time they learned.

As different as these groups are, they have two things in common. First, in each case, they were motivated by a challenging, compelling vision. None of them would describe their work as meaningless or boring. Second, they acted. Even NASA, with their long, deliberate planning process, eventually pushes the button to launch the rocket.

These are the people we know about, but there is a third invisible category. They aren't like an engineering team planning a space mission, and they aren't courageous explorers. They're the ones who don't do anything. Whether due to fear or lack of opportunity, many unnamed people choose safety even as others venture out.

Despite all the advances in technology and access to information, today's context for ministry leadership more closely resembles that of the early explorers. We don't have NASA-like resources to declare "Failure is not an option," nor are we dealing with problems that can be solved conclusively with bright people and powerful computers. Instead, the challenge is to lead others into a future filled with uncertainty or, as Robert Quinn says, "to build the bridge as we walk on it."*

This is a scary way to lead. But if engineering a perfect solution is not feasible, then we're faced with either leading into the unknown or not leading at all. I don't think you'd be reading this book if you prefer the latter option. Equally important is that the people in your church expect you to lead, and God is calling you to do so.

That leaves us with the question of where to lead. You may not have the clarion call of leaving footprints on the moon by the end of a decade, but you can develop a picture of God's preferred future for your church or ministry. And with that picture in mind, you can take the right next step.

It Starts with Vision

Every church or ministry needs a vision, a description of their best understanding of God's preferred future. You may have had disappointing experiences in the past with a vision that produced little fruit. But the alternative—no vision at all—will certainly not lead your church toward a brighter and more vibrant future. The people

---

* Quinn, *Deep Change*, 84.

in your church want to know they're going somewhere. If they wanted to go on a ride that returned them to their starting point, they'd go to an amusement park.

The process for discerning vision is the subject of numerous books and is beyond the scope of this chapter. But it is important to understand what vision is and what it isn't. Vision is a "clear, shared, and compelling picture of the preferred future to which God is calling your congregation"* (or ministry). The "shared" element will be explored in perspective 4, but what about "clear and compelling"?

Instead of using the single word *clear*, it's more helpful to say a vision needs to be *clear enough*. The addition of the word *enough* is an important qualifier. A vision that is too vague results in puzzled looks—"What does that mean?" Or it may result in no looks at all, just blank stares of indifference. Your church may have a vision to change the world, but so does every other church and ministry and nonprofit. If your vision doesn't say something about your unique place in changing the world, it is likely to fall flat.

At the same time, *clear enough* gives a leader permission to not know all the details, especially in the early stages of articulating and pursuing a vision. Leaders don't need to be able to answer every question about *how* the vision will be achieved. They may not even be completely accurate as they paint a picture of what reaching the vision will look like.

First Church's vision was to "change the world, one life at a time, beginning at our side doors." Many churches want to change the world, so the two extra phrases were an important distinction for First. Several years earlier, the church made an intentional decision to stay downtown, rather than moving, because they believed God was calling them to have a vibrant ministry in the center of their midsize city. The church's imposing front entrance seemed designed for devout Christians in their Sunday finest, so the leadership team

---

* Jim Herrington, Mike Bonem, and James H. Furr, *Leading Congregational Change: A Practical Guide for the Transformational Journey* (Minneapolis: Fortress, 2020), 49.

coined the phrase "side door" to indicate their desire to reach a broader group of people. "One life at a time" emphasized the importance of individual relationships rather than large attractional events.

As First Church's leaders continued to develop the vision, they realized the church had two important side doors to explore. One door was for people in the business community who worked Monday through Friday in the blocks surrounding the church. The other side door was for the people who lived within half a mile of the church, just to the east of downtown. Several low-income apartment complexes in this area were home to a large number of refugees and immigrants. The leadership team had not determined how they would reach out to these two groups, but they were satisfied that the vision was clear enough to begin making initial plans.

Compelling describes the potency of the vision. Advertisements for pickup trucks often show them moving incredibly heavy loads. The message is, "If you have a big job to do, you want our truck." A compelling vision does the heavy work of moving people forward. People want to be on a winning team. They want their church to have a positive impact on their community and the world. A compelling vision creates excitement and anticipation about the church's future. It translates into energy that moves people into action.

Lewis and Clark's exploration of the newly acquired Louisiana Territory is a powerful example of a vision that was compelling and clear enough. For years, experts had been convinced of the existence of an all-water route across North America. They knew discovering this route would have enormous benefits. The vision for Lewis and Clark was to create a firsthand account of the country's newly acquired territory and find the best route for reaching the Pacific Northwest. That vision was compelling and clear enough to motivate a group of people to make a harrowing, two-and-a-half-year expedition that captured the attention of an entire nation. When Lewis and Clark reached the headwaters of the Missouri River and realized the all-water route didn't exist, they didn't give up. Instead, they refined their understanding of the vision and how they would pursue it.*

Think of this as leading with a compass, not a map. A map implies knowing the exact destination and every step to be taken along the route. Today we just need to turn on the location services and input an address, and our phone navigates wherever we want to go. But what if you only knew that your destination was 500 miles to the west and didn't have a phone or a detailed map? This is the analogy for leading a church or ministry today. It's certainly where Lewis and Clark found themselves at that critical point in their journey. To reach that destination, those early explorers and leaders today must take the first step.

Taking the First Step

Some of the most familiar stories in the Bible are based on a vision that barely seems clear enough, and yet the leader steps out in faith. Abraham wasn't given a destination. He was simply told to leave his country and go to a land that God would show him. Joshua crossed the Jordan with knowledge of the land but without a battle plan for how to conquer it. Paul's well-known vision of a man in Macedonia was compelling enough to change his immediate plans, but it didn't include a list of cities to visit or a guide for enduring opposition and persecution.

Even one of the greatest vision commands in Scripture, the Great Commission, is thin on details: "Therefore go and make disciples of all nations, baptizing them in the name of the Father and of the Son and of the Holy Spirit, and teaching them to obey everything I have commanded you" (Matt 28:19–20). Questions such as

---

* Tod Bolsinger's *Canoeing the Mountains* is an outstanding book on leading into an unknown and uncertain future. Bolsinger follows the Lewis and Clark story to identify many powerful applications for church leaders.

"Where do we begin?" or "How can our small band do this?" were unanswered. Despite the many questions that today's leaders might ask in similar situations, these visions were clear enough for God's chosen leaders to take a first step, trusting that God would show them the next steps at the proper time.

There's a reason we have so many sayings like "A journey of a thousand miles begins with a single step" or "God can't steer a parked car." These statements highlight the value of creating movement. They recognize the inertia that can keep a person or organization frozen in place. The scientific principle of inertia, Newton's first law of motion, states that an object at rest will stay at rest unless acted on by another force. Leaders need to be aware of the power of organizational inertia. A church or ministry will remain at rest unless acted on by a force of leadership.

As most organizations approach the point of action, their leaders must choose between several possible first steps. As a leader, you probably won't make a unilateral decision about which path to follow, but your influence on the decision is important. When possible, look for ways to take small steps at the beginning. Small steps are usually less visible, encounter less resistance, and can build momentum for bigger steps. (Perspective 7 examines this in detail.)

First Church's leaders were thinking of small steps as they developed the initial plans to move toward their vision. For the downtown business community, the church decided to launch a weekly midweek Bible study during the lunch hour. They encouraged church members who worked downtown to come and invite coworkers. Even though 25 people came to the first meeting, all but three of them were church members, and two of those were actively involved in other churches. Little changed over the rest of the semester, leaving the leadership team to reevaluate the effectiveness of this first step.

For the nearby immigrant community, First Church decided its first step would be to offer ESL (English as a Second Language) classes one night a week. Despite several creative efforts at getting the word out, the class never attracted more than four people. As the leaders investigated further, they learned that several community organizations were already offering ESL on-site at the nearby apartments. That same investigation, however, revealed a significant need for job training and job placement for the apartment residents. The church shifted its focus, partnering with a local nonprofit and enlisting several retired businesspeople to spearhead these efforts, which quickly grew to an average of 40 participants each week.

These stories illustrate the fluid nature of first steps. Success is not guaranteed, especially when trying something new and unproven. The art of leading change requires a leader to diligently pursue a vision while at the same time holding specific plans loosely and making adjustments along the way.

Leaders must also be able to step back and honestly evaluate the results of new initiatives. The number of participants in the midweek Bible study might tempt a leader to claim success rather than admitting it didn't achieve the goal of reaching unchurched people. Someone might even defend the ESL program by saying, "Isn't it worth doing if we reach just one person?" Of course, the ability to conduct meaningful evaluations is only possible if concrete goals are established in advance.

When choosing which steps to take first, wise leaders resist the urge to overcommit. Typical planning processes generate a basketful of good ideas to move a church toward a vision. This leads to the question: What will we do first? Earlier in First Church's planning, the leadership team brainstormed a wide range of possibilities for their side doors. But they narrowed their target audience to just two groups, and they initially launched one new initiative for each. When each idea has great potential and a champion on the leadership team, it can be difficult to pick one. But it's far better to have the hard conversations leading to a focused effort than to attempt multiple initiatives that dilute resources and confuse the congregation.

Both of First Church's initial steps were relatively modest, but what if a small first step is not an option? The church wasn't ready to give up on the vision of reaching downtown workers, despite their disappointment with the weekday Bible study. One church member, who was also a leader in the city's chamber of commerce, suggested a monthly luncheon featuring guest speakers who would address different topics related to leadership in the workplace. The idea was very attractive, especially with the chamber of commerce as a cosponsor, but it wasn't easy to implement. The level of preparation and the financial cost were much greater than those for a simple Bible study. A group of church members was upset that some of the proposed speakers were not Christian. And some people who had never been excited about the focus on the church's "side doors" used the Bible study's "failure" as evidence that the entire emphasis should be scrapped.

Leaders should always be realistic about the cost of change, especially when the changes are significant. *Cost* is much more than the financial resources needed for the new undertaking. It also includes time and energy that leaders and volunteers must give to the effort and the emotional toll of dealing with resistance. Whenever the first step is a big step, a strong leadership team is essential (as we will see in perspective 4). And regardless of whether the first step is big or small, leaders need to be prepared to encounter obstacles before they take a single step.

Obstacles to Taking the First Step

Given their incredible success, it is striking how little Lewis and Clark knew before starting their expedition. They didn't know whether the Native Americans they'd encounter would be friendly or hostile. They didn't know whether they'd be able to find food easily on the journey. They certainly didn't know about the intense and formidable mountains that would stand in their way. But despite their ignorance, they made the best plans they could and set out on their journey in the spring of 1804.

If the decisions about the expedition had been in the hands of a typical church committee, Lewis and Clark would have left in 1805 or 1806, or maybe not at all. I am not an advocate for a ready-fire-aim approach to leadership. But I would prefer a leader who is a little trigger-happy over one with the tendency for ready-aim-aim-aim-aim-aim. . . . That is why it is important to understand and overcome the obstacles that can prevent your church from taking the first steps toward a vision.

A leader's own fear of conflict is one common obstacle, as is the associated desire to have unanimous support for new proposals. In these cases, leaders delay acting even though they have enough support to move forward. This is such a common and important issue that an entire chapter is devoted to it (perspective 5).

Several other obstacles have nothing to do with the leader's desire to keep everyone happy but instead are part of the fabric of the church. Some congregations have a NASA mindset that tries to engineer failure-proof plans. It's good to think about what could go wrong and identify the possible unintended consequences of a new program. There may even be times when it seems that God is saying "wait" or "not yet." Just be aware that the good intention to plan thoughtfully can become a paralyzing tendency to analyze endlessly.

If a church is prone to overengineered solutions, the leader's job is to name this and propose a different mindset. You can invite the leadership team to be satisfied with a "90% solution," a plan that is well designed but doesn't try to anticipate every possible contingency. The team may need to be reminded that no plan is guaranteed to succeed. They may need to see that going from a 90% to a 99% solution requires significant effort to produce only modest gains.

Similarly, a culture of "endless discussions" can prevent the first step from happening. Some leadership teams have a habit of talking about an issue, then talking more and more, sometimes chasing rabbits and never reaching a decision. It isn't an issue of overengineering as much as a lack of focus. Gentle but firm facilitation of team meetings, along with clarity about what decisions need to be made now, can reshape this frustrating tendency.

Of course, it's easier to have endless discussions when leaders lack urgency. One of the most common reasons for a lack of urgency is a vision that is not compelling or clear enough. A vibrant vision needs to address a real issue that is tangible and that people care about. And it needs to point out the gap between the church's current reality and its vision.

When leaders at First Church began talking about the vision to reach the downtown business community through their "side doors," some church members were skeptical: "Shouldn't we focus on building Sunday worship attendance?" "People are downtown during the week for work; they're not thinking about spiritual questions." "I don't know anyone at work who is looking for a church." The lack of urgency behind these comments seemed like it might derail the vision.

Then one Sunday, the congregation heard Hannah's testimony. She described being raised in a Christian home but wandering from faith as a young adult. She was excited when she was hired by the leading ad agency in town. But after just a couple of years, the work was less fulfilling, and she felt a deep sense of loneliness and emptiness in her life. She said,

> I thought about coming here on a Sunday, but I didn't even know where to start. Then one Tuesday as I walked by the church on my lunch break, I felt this invisible tug to go inside. I wandered into the chapel and sat down to pray. I had no idea what to say. As I sat there, one of the pastors came in and offered to pray with me. That was the beginning of a dramatic change in my life. I'm so thankful the doors were open that day. I doubt I would have had the courage to come on a Sunday.

Creating the urgency to overcome obstacles can take many forms. It may be a story like Hannah's, an analysis that demonstrates the opportunity, or a small group of passionate leaders who won't be stopped.

The skeptics at First Church, and in your church, can be some of the biggest obstacles to a first step of change. One of the most tenuous moments in the journey of change is in the prelaunch stage. The concerns raised by the members at First Church were legitimate. They needed to be taken seriously. The art of leading change is allowing enough time and space to address these questions, without allowing the entire process to be held hostage by a small group of people who will never be supportive.

Ultimately, overcoming the obstacles to taking a first step is also a spiritual issue. The guidance of the Holy Spirit informs the decisions about which steps to take and gives leaders the conviction to press ahead as they encounter hurdles. Without this conviction, leaders are prone to hesitation and doubt. Even with the Spirit's guidance and a clear and compelling vision, leaders may be slow to act because they feel overwhelmed. The overarching dream may be daunting, and the best way to start may be uncertain. And yet that's the moment when a leader needs to step up and step out, nudging the people to take a first step in faith.

Beyond the First Step

Leading your church to take a first step is essential. There can't be a change journey without it. But don't make the "silver bullet" mistake of thinking that you can get to your destination in just one step or that leadership challenges dissolve once you start moving. Successful change leaders know that the first step is just that—the first of many on their way toward a compelling vision of God's preferred future for their church or ministry.

A baby's first step is a celebrated moment, and rightly so. Excited parents reach for their phones to record the milestone. They call friends and family members to share the news. But a parent would never stop at that point and proclaim their job was done. The same should be true for pastors and ministry leaders. Yes, take the time to celebrate a first step in the change process. This is a great opportunity to build momentum through intentional communication. But don't stop there.

The progression after a baby's first step is predictable. They falter less, they walk farther and faster, and eventually they begin to run. In the same way, ministry leaders should always be thinking about their right next step. It may not be as obvious or predictable as for a baby. But clarity of vision, attentiveness to the Holy Spirit, and deliberate evaluation of options can guide the choice of next steps just as they did for the first steps.

Taking the right next steps also requires leaders to display the same attributes that catalyzed the first steps: a bias toward action, a willingness to try and fail and learn, and the determination to press ahead in the face of opposition. A toddler doesn't stop falling after taking their first steps. In fact, the bumps and bruises may get even worse as they begin to run and jump. But it's the only way they can continue to develop. In the same way, you will continue to encounter setbacks and disappointments in your journey as a change leader, but you must not let that keep you from taking the right next step.

FROM PERSPECTIVE TO PRACTICE

TAKE THE RIGHT NEXT STEP

- Evaluate your church or ministry's vision. Is it clear enough? Is it compelling? If not, what needs to change?
- If the vision is clear enough, what first steps should your church consider? Develop a plan to move from imagining those steps to taking them.

- Invite your leadership team to evaluate the way your church or ministry does planning. Did this perspective highlight any deficiencies in the process that need to be addressed?
- What aspects of your personality make it difficult to take a first step? Or, conversely, if you're quick to step out, what do you need to guard against?

Heavy Loads Require Strong Teams

I magine that you are an artist who has received a commission to create a sculpture for your city's premier outdoor park. Your business partner offers to handle all the logistics so that you can focus on the creative process. After several months, you're thrilled to have the finished piece in your warehouse studio and can't wait for its public unveiling. Your partner shows up with a small pickup truck, which is totally inadequate for transporting the five-ton sculpture. When you ask about the crew for the installation in the park, you discover he only arranged for two people to be there and no heavy equipment.

This scene borders on absurd, right? The value of the artwork is in displaying it for the public. No one would do the hard work of creating a sculpture without having a way to move it out of the studio. And yet that is exactly what some leaders do on the path toward change for their church or ministry.

The principle in this chapter—*heavy loads require strong teams*—is simple. The bigger or heavier the load represented by a potential change, the stronger the team needed to carry it to completion. "Heavier" can mean several things. It may refer to the scope of the proposed change and the number of people who will be affected. A renovation project for an entire facility is a "heavier load" than redecorating the youth area.

Heavier can refer to the financial and other resources that are needed to make the change happen. When the budget is tight, adding communication and technology staff to support a new digital outreach strategy is a big change. The anticipated amount of resistance also makes a change feel heavy. If a pastor decides to spend more time on community outreach than on leading the small midweek Bible study, the outcry may be surprisingly loud.

Heavy loads require strong teams. That much is obvious. The art of leading change is in assessing the weight of the challenge that lies ahead and then recruiting and developing the teams to carry the load across the finish line.

Count the Cost

Jesus tells a parable about the importance of counting the cost:

> Suppose one of you wants to build a tower. Won't you first sit down and estimate the cost to see if you have enough money to complete it? For if you lay the foundation and are not able to finish it, everyone who sees it will ridicule you, saying, "This person began to build and wasn't able to finish." (Luke 14:28–30)

Jesus taught this parable about the cost of being his disciple, but shouldn't leaders also apply the wisdom of counting the cost to the steps they are taking to make disciples? What is the cost of the changes that are on the horizon?

You've heard the adage "There's no such thing as a free lunch." The leadership equivalent is that every change comes with a cost. Don't think that proposed changes will sail through simply because of compelling rationale, or a unanimous vote by the governing board, or your personal charisma and close relationships. All of those factors may lower the cost and make success more likely, but every change has its price.

The costs for a proposed change or new initiative can include many elements, but they fall into four general categories: financial resources, nonfinancial resources, opportunity cost, and resistance. The financial costs are the most obvious and simplest to calculate. It's easy to get a handle on programming expenses or the cost of new staff. The next two categories are often underemphasized or overlooked. Nonfinancial resources include the time that must be given by volunteers and existing staff members for a change to get off the ground. Opportunity cost recognizes that a church does not have an endless supply of financial and volunteer resources. Saying yes to a new idea also means a silent no to a different one.

The first three categories are important, but the one that can be the most damaging is resistance to change. When people within the church don't like a proposed change, they may oppose it directly, which requires time and energy to address. Or they may simply leave the church, resulting in a loss of volunteers and financial support. A strong team will not prevent resistance from occurring, but the skills and wisdom they bring to address resistance can reduce this cost.

After a season of discernment, the elders of Sunnyside Church concluded their congregation was too inwardly focused. Casey, their pastor, wanted to lead the way in building bridges with the community, and he realized that one of the biggest obstacles was the amount of time he spent on pastoral care. He knew the needs of the members couldn't be neglected, so he and the elders agreed to create a volunteer care team and reduce the time he personally spent on hospital visitation and counseling.

Casey led the elders in a lengthy discussion of what this shift would cost. They estimated that the volunteer care team would need two coleaders and at least ten other people. Casey's administrative assistant would spend about five hours a week coordinating the communication related to care needs. The financial impact of the new system was negligible. The most difficult cost to estimate was the negative fallout from the congregation, especially the older members. Casey and the elders planned several meetings to answer questions, and they felt confident that the strong support from the elders combined with a well-designed plan would calm any fears.

Every change brings unintended consequences, which is one of the most difficult parts of counting the cost. Sometimes these are good. Sunnyside can celebrate if the shift in the pastoral care strategy causes existing groups to take more responsibility to care for their members. But in the context of cost counting, it's the negative, unintended consequences that can derail the change effort. What will happen if Sunnyside's new care team doesn't feel adequately prepared for their role? Or if the changes actually increase the number of requests for pastoral care beyond their capacity? If the new system can't meet the congregation's needs, pressure will build to revert to a pastor-centric model of care.

It's a mistake to launch a major change without considering the full range of costs that are likely to be incurred. Calculating the cost for a change is much more than an accounting exercise. You don't need that degree of precision, but you do need to consider a variety of factors. As you count the costs, you'll realize the need for strong teams to help carry the load.

Teams That Make Decisions

Implementing a major change always involves many different people. For example, a church that is launching a new campus needs people to greet guests, make coffee, teach children, and participate on the worship team. All these individuals and their activities are important, but they are all part of *doing* the change. As you think about the strong teams that are needed to lift heavy loads, the focus should be the people who are *leading* change. And they fall into two distinct groups: those who decide which changes to pursue and those who plan and implement the specific initiatives.

The group charged with making the big, strategic decisions is usually easy to define. It's the governing body or executive team of your church or ministry. You can stop and name these individuals right now. But even though they can be readily identified, it does not mean that you have the right people on the team or that their interactions are leading to the best decisions.

The ideal group for making major decisions has several characteristics. They are spiritually mature and are committed to seeking God's direction (see perspective 10). They represent a cross section of the church. They engage in meetings, not as representatives of a constituent group, but as leaders trying to make the best decisions for the entire organization. When you think of a good cross section, you may think of different ministry areas or of age, gender, and ethnic diversity. But the ideal mix also includes people with different perspectives and who have been part of the church for varying lengths of time. The team should include people who are dreamers and ones who are cautious and practical.

Consider adding people to the decision-making team who are not deeply tied to "how we've always done things." Examples might include individuals who are newer to the church, who simply have not been in leadership roles, or those who are naturally creative, out-of-the-box thinkers. They may exasperate a group by frequently asking questions, but their curiosity and their suggestions often lead to new options and ultimately to better decisions.

When Sunnyside's elders first began discussing their desire for the church to turn outward, Brendan, one of the newest to the group, spoke up: "We will never reach our vision if we don't reach into our community more. Casey, it's not all on your shoulders, but as our pastor, you need to lead the way. What are the barriers? What fills up most of your calendar?" Casey answered that sermon preparation and congregational care were the two biggest blocks of time during his work week. Brendan's response changed the direction of the meeting: "We certainly don't want you to shortcut your sermons, but why does the pastor have to do so much congregational care?" Several other elders were quick to say that this "pastoral work" couldn't be done by volunteers, but Brendan persisted, asking if all congregational care had to be done by a clergy person. Over the course of the next two meetings, the idea for the volunteer care team began to emerge.

A decision-making body that includes a wide variety of perspectives may sound large, but the best ones have 12 or fewer people. The right dozen can bring enough different viewpoints, and more importantly, they can have productive conversations. What is "productive"? It's when a strategic decision is carefully examined from multiple angles and the merits are debated. This doesn't happen when the decision-making group is too large or too like-minded. That kind of group tends to either rubber-stamp the recommendation of the pastor or get stuck in endless discussions that go nowhere.

The willingness and ability to have productive conversations is not just a function of who is in the group or its size. It is also determined by the unseen norms. Is it OK to voice disagreement? What happens when someone offers a different perspective from the pastor or the group's leader?

When Brendan joined the elder board at Sunnyside, he spent the first meeting quietly observing the group dynamics. When Casey made a proposal, the back-and-forth discussion that followed was both energetic and respectful. Brendan concluded that healthy debate was acceptable in the meetings, so he wasn't hesitant to challenge the assumptions about congregational care a few months later. But what would have happened if he had observed an atmosphere where contrary opinions and alternative views were never expressed? It's unlikely he would have raised his question.

This tendency to be nice and go along will never result in a strong team that can carry a heavy load. For the teams charged with decision-making, carrying the load means choosing which path is best *and* fully supporting the decision once it is made public. If a team member doesn't voice concerns because the group norms discourage questions, how will she respond when a friend asks for her opinion about the proposal? Her response is likely to be tepid at best, and it might be outright critical.

Productive decision-making conversations involve the right kind of debate. Just like some churches have norms that squelch disagreement, others make a habit of unhealthy conflict. Healthy debate focuses on the issue and respects the views of others. Unhealthy conflict builds defensive positions and disrespects or even attacks those who are not in agreement. Developing a set of written group norms and then holding one another accountable to those norms can help combat tendencies to be too ugly or too nice.

The bottom line is that you need the right size group with the right people discussing the right issues in the right ways. It's a lot to get right, but it's essential when significant changes are on the horizon.

Teams That Implement Change

Making wise, strategic decisions is important, but changes won't occur unless someone plans and implements them. You probably have had at least one experience when a great idea didn't get off the ground. The failure is often due to a lack of adequate leadership for the new initiative. This is the second place where strong teams are essential.

After Sunnyside's elders agreed to create the volunteer care team and shift Casey's responsibilities, the real work began. Two people were recruited to lead the team. One was a longtime church member who was organized and detail oriented. The other, one of Sunnyside's newer members, had caught the attention of several leaders as a person with great relational skills and tremendous compassion for people in need. Casey's assistant was asked to be part of the leadership meetings to help facilitate important linkages with the church's care systems. And Casey regularly joined these three leaders to help them plan and launch the new initiative.

The care team leaders met weekly to work out the many details. These included identifying and recruiting potential team members, setting expectations for care, developing training for the yet-to-be-formed team, creating systems to track and communicate congregational care needs, and determining the types of needs that required pastoral involvement. The leaders also mapped out a plan for communicating the new approach to the congregation. When the new care ministry launched, it exceeded everyone's expectations, thanks largely to the hard work of the team leaders. There were a few missteps, but these were quickly addressed in ways that improved congregational care at Sunnyside even more.

This example highlights several important factors about the kinds of teams that lead effective change. The best way to successfully launch a new initiative is with a small, dedicated leadership team with diverse skills. They need to work closely together to plan the details and accomplish the various tasks. The team could be as small as three people when the effort is modest and as large as eight to ten people for a large undertaking.

Implementing change requires leadership, but it's a different kind of leadership than the high-level decisions described in the previous section. Planning and implementation call for strategic and tactical thinking, seeing both the forest and the trees. This kind of leadership is time and labor intensive. It is task and people oriented. In other words, it is not a job for a solo leader or for people who are already overcommitted.

Rather than going to the "usual suspects," those tireless and tired individuals who are always asked to lead, this is a great opportunity to recruit some fresh faces. But don't make the mistake of thinking anyone can do this job. There are many people who will be able to contribute as doers for the new initiative, and their roles are important. At this point, however, you need passionate *leaders*, so look for people who have leadership experience, whether in the church or elsewhere. The PTO president or the person who leads a small project development team at work has valuable skills that can be used for your change effort. Look for people whose eyes light up when you talk about the specific need that is being addressed. If ministry for vulnerable children is what energizes someone, don't ask them to lead the volunteer care team. They might say yes to the request out of loyalty to the church or relationship with the pastor, but they won't give their best efforts to something that fails to stir a fire deep within their soul.

If putting this team together sounds like the straightforward science of leading change, think again. The art is finding and recruiting the right mix of personalities and skills to form a powerful team. It is knowing how much freedom to give the team and when to get involved. It is anticipating places where they may need additional resources or support.

For the change to succeed, you will need to stay connected with the work being done by this leadership group. Are the emerging plans consistent with the vision, or might a slight course correction be needed? What early successes can you amplify to encourage the team and build momentum (as described in perspective 7)? How does the resistance they encounter need to be addressed? The ability to deal with such resistance is the true test of strength for any leadership team.

Passing the Strength Test

If you see a newcomer to the gym, you may have a guess about their strength just by looking at the size of their muscles. But you don't truly know their strength until you see the amount of weight they lift.

In the same way, you can have a team—for making decisions or for planning and leading a change initiative—that appears to be outstanding, but you won't know their real strength until they are tested. And the real test for leadership teams in church or ministry settings is when they encounter setbacks or resistance, especially opposition from within the congregation. When fellow church members object to the change, how will these leaders respond? This is a critical moment for change efforts. If leaders change their minds in the face of disagreement, or even if they step to the side and watch in silence, the effort will be derailed.

Sunnyside's elders anticipated that some people would not be happy with the creation of the volunteer care team. The elders calmly answered questions in a congregational meeting where the proposal was presented and even diffused a couple of angry comments. The real test occurred the following week when one of the elders went to her regular Bible study. Before the class began, several people surrounded her and asked pointedly if she really believed the care team proposal would work. To her credit, she didn't back down, even though she could tell that her friends were displeased with her response.

The change journey is full of twists and turns, and nothing can guarantee success, but there are ways to improve the odds that key teams won't wilt in the face of opposition. The first way is to avoid misinterpreting a positive vote or nodding heads. The board may say they are in favor of a proposed change and the planning team may seem ready to launch the program, but that does not mean they are fully committed. They may simply be convinced by a leader's eloquence, or they may not have spent enough time considering all the possibilities.

The key word in the previous paragraph is *committed*. There is a world of difference between someone who doesn't vote against a proposal and someone who is truly committed to it. Committed people have a high level of buy-in and ownership. They use first-person plural pronouns to refer to the change initiative—"the changes that *we* are making" or "*our* plans"—not third-person pronouns that keep them at arm's length from any fallout.

Positive votes and excitement can be generated by a powerful speech or by a convincing presentation, but commitment requires a deeper and more thoughtful approach. As described earlier in this chapter, disagreement is a surprisingly powerful tool for building commitment. When a leadership team is considering a significant change, differing opinions should be expected. A leader's job is to make room for those opinions to be expressed and explored. Allowing the time and space for healthy debate is one of the best means for achieving commitment to the ultimate decisions.

In the debate over a proposed change, someone will inevitably point out the risks or downsides of the idea, including the possibility of opposition. A robust conversation about how the church will react and who might resist can lead to better decisions and a stronger team. Plans can be adjusted to address the anticipated concerns. Even if a concern can't be resolved, leaders can be better prepared to respond to the pushback. Either way, the discussion within the leadership team will better equip them to carry the change to completion.

It takes time to build strong teams that can carry heavy loads. When leaders feel pulled in many directions (which is most of the time), they may be tempted to forge ahead with a weak team or question the need for a team altogether. Some leaders decide that sharing leadership with a team just isn't worth the time and effort. Some leaders worry about the loss of control that will occur when they release a team to plan and implement a major change.

At Sunnyside, Casey experienced moments of anxiety about the care team. The planning stage increased the demands on his time as he met regularly with the team leaders and continued to do the majority of the congregational care. He also worried that the quality of congregational care would suffer or that the volunteers would fail to ask for help in crisis situations. Whenever these voices of doubt became too loud, he reminded himself of Brendan's challenge.

Developing strong teams is no small task, but it is an essential one. Going back to the analogy at the start of this chapter, trying to lead change without those teams would be like creating a sculpture without a way to display it. The piece of art might be beautiful, but only a few people will ever see it unless a way is found to move it out of the artist's studio. When preparing for a big change, never forget that great ideas are of little value without the strong teams to carry them to the finish line.

FROM PERSPECTIVE TO PRACTICE

HEAVY LOADS REQUIRE STRONG TEAMS

- Reflect on your own leadership style. Do you believe the central message of this perspective? What in your personality and past experiences may cause you to be reluctant to use teams for making key decisions and for leading major initiatives? Invite a trusted friend to share insights into these questions.
- Evaluate your current governing body based on the ideas in this perspective. Do you have the right people? Do you have productive conversations? Can they make weighty decisions?
- Think about a change initiative that is in the works. What kind of leadership team will enable this initiative to soar? Who are the best candidates to lead that team?
- What are you doing to prepare key teams to deal effectively with setbacks and resistance?

AN Artist's PERSPECTIVE

The Science Behind the Art

The introduction to this book makes a sharp distinction between the science and the art of leading change. We tend to think of science as objective and art as subjective. Science is full of factual principles that are not open for debate or alternative interpretations. With art, we use expressions that underscore its subjectivity, such as "Beauty is in the eye of the beholder." But it turns out that art has a great deal of science supporting it.

What would you think if you saw a portrait in which the subject's different body parts were out of proportion? One arm longer than the other, the legs far too short compared to the torso, the head formed into an odd triangular shape. Unless the artist intended to create an abstract expression, you would think the painting was destined for the garbage and not for display.

It turns out, the human body has certain predictable proportions that should guide any portrait artist. The face is symmetrical along a vertical axis that runs from the forehead, down the nose, to the chin. The eyes are at the midpoint of this vertical line. The distance between the inside corners of the eyes is the width of one eye. The outer edges of the mouth align with the centers of the eyes. The tops of the ears are at the same level as the eyes.[*] Ignoring this "science" will produce a distasteful result.

---

[*] Betty Edwards, *Drawing on the Right Side of the Brain* (New York: St. Martin's, 1989), 143–44.

A similar analysis of proportions could be done for the rest of the human body, for animals, and for almost anything else an artist might want to draw. There's also science behind the mixing of colors for a painting, the arrangement of notes in a chord, and the number of revolutions a ballet dancer makes as she spins on her toes.

This is not to suggest in any way that creating a work of art is a mechanical exercise that can be done by anyone who understands the science. The science just provides a foundation on which the artist can build. Ask three artists to paint the same seascape and you'll get three different expressions. But they will all draw on scientific principles related to perspective, light, and color.

In the same way, the art of leading people through change can have a variety of expressions, even for similar contexts. There are likely to be different opinions on what constitutes a "beautiful" outcome. But when you examine ministry leadership that produces meaningful organizational change, you're sure to find important principles at work. Ignore these principles and the outcome will not be beautiful, regardless of the beholder.

PERSPECTIVE 5

You Can't Please Everyone

You can please all the people some of the time and some of the people all the time, but you cannot please all the people all the time. No, that's not the exact quote attributed to Abraham Lincoln. He referred to fooling the people, not pleasing them. But when it comes to leading change, this riff on Lincoln's words is an essential perspective for leaders to keep in mind.

What's funny about this statement is that pastors and ministry leaders readily agree that keeping everyone happy all the time is impossible. And yet time after time, the process of meaningful change is slowed, interrupted, or completely stopped by a leader's desire to please everyone.

A vivid picture of this reality about pleasing people is found in John 6. The feeding of the five thousand is recorded in all four Gospels. It was a moment when all the people were pleased because they had witnessed a miracle and their stomachs were full. Immediately afterward they said, "Surely this is the Prophet who is to come into the world" (John 6:14).

But just a short time later, Jesus taught his followers that he was the bread of life (John 6:25–59). The response was much less enthusiastic: "Many of his disciples said, 'This is a hard teaching. Who can accept it?'" (John 6:60). But they didn't just question his teaching: "From this time many of his disciples turned back and no longer followed him" (John 6:66). If history's greatest leader knew that he couldn't (and shouldn't) please everyone all the time, why should any of the rest of us think we can?

Even though pleasing everyone is an unrealistic expectation, some level of support and approval is essential for any new initiative. So what does it mean to "please people" in the context of leading change? It is more than getting a thumbs-up based on personal approval. It is not catering to a consumer mindset and giving them whatever they want, even though people's desires do need to be considered. These are contributing factors, but in this chapter, pleasing people refers to *building enough genuine support that a major change effort can move forward*. The hard work of change doesn't call for pleasing everyone, but it does require the commitment of enough of the right people.

Who Can You Please?

It's not difficult to imagine those moments when a leader can please all, or almost all, the people. If all the external measures are positive, people are generally pleased. In moments of celebration—a full church on Easter, the baptism service for several new members, the report from a life-changing mission trip—smiles will be seen throughout the congregation. It might be a slight overstatement to say that everyone is pleased at these times—every congregation has that grouchy curmudgeon whose face is frozen in a permanent frown—but these are certainly moments when leaders feel the wind at their backs.

It's also easy to think of individuals who are always pleased and supportive of your leadership. They are the perpetual optimists who don't just think of the glass as half-full but find ways to see it as filled to the brim. They are gentle souls who never say a negative word about anyone. Or they may be people who have become close friends and will stick with you through thick and thin. With these people, you've never preached a bad sermon. You've never made bad decisions;

you've just had some opportunities to learn. These individuals are an important part of a leader's life, but they're not a helpful barometer for assessing the obstacles on the change journey.

So if you can ignore the occasional curmudgeon and love but can't rely on the people who are always pleased, who is left? A lot of people. They're the ones who will be pleased some of the time, and they're the group that needs to be examined more closely.

In his theory on the "diffusion of innovations," Everett Rogers divides people into five groups: innovators, early adopters, early majority, late majority, and laggards.* These are listed in the order in which they will buy or accept a new product, service, or idea. Innovators are the people who stood in line for the first iPhones or were the earliest users of TikTok. In contrast, the laggards are the last ones to make the shift, and sometimes never do so. You can probably think of someone who didn't have a smartphone for years after they became available, not because of financial reasons or a lack of technological capability, but just because they didn't see the point in having an internet-connected device in the palm of their hand.

Every leader has experienced these different categories in their church or ministry. Even a bad idea will have some supporters. Even a good idea will have people who want more information or evidence before they get on board. And even the greatest idea, one that seems like a slam dunk, will run into some opposition. *There will always be laggards* in any significant change effort.

Elizabeth, the founding pastor of Redemption Church, was experiencing this reality firsthand. When Elizabeth initially sensed God calling her to plant a new church, several friends advised her to reconsider. But she was confident that the dream of a new, vibrant downtown church was led by the Spirit. After five years of hard work, the dream was coming true. The church's weekly worship service was nearing the capacity of the venue they rented on

---

* Everett M. Rogers, *Diffusion of Innovations* (New York: Free Press, 2003). The concept was originally published in the 1962 edition of this book.

Sundays, so Elizabeth and the leadership team were planning for a second service.

But capacity wasn't the only limiting factor with the space. The venue was only available on Sunday mornings and the rooms available for children were less than ideal. Then a realtor told Elizabeth about a nearby commercial building that was about to go on the market. After several weeks of negotiations, Redemption's leadership team had agreed to terms on a deal for the building. Significant renovations would be required, and the cost would stretch the church's finances, but it seemed like they had found a great option for a permanent home that would allow the church to continue to grow.

Completing the purchase would require a vote of the congregation, so the next step was to announce the proposed deal and allow time for input from the church's members. Not surprisingly, there were a variety of reactions. Some people were immediately excited. They saw great potential in having a permanent space, including the opportunities to expand ministry, provide better children's spaces, and escape the drudgery of weekly setups. Other people were uncertain. They had questions about the finances, the attractiveness of the new location, and other factors. And a few people were staunchly opposed to the proposal. Some of them didn't think the church should ever own property. Others believed the move was premature. The middle group of uncertain people is similar to the "early and late majorities" in Rogers's theory. Elizabeth knew the proposal needed their support, and she was committed to answering their questions and allowing them time for reflection before scheduling a vote. But what about the ones who expressed direct opposition? Should the church try to win over these "laggards"?

The Risk of Trying to Please Everyone

At this point, you may wonder about the meaning of *laggard* in this context. After all, the word doesn't suggest someone who is actively working against a proposed change. It just implies a person who is slow to come around to a new idea. This leads to the natural question, "Shouldn't we give the laggards time to get on board?" Probably not. But understanding this answer requires taking a closer look at the people who are not easily pleased and the risks of trying to please everyone.

Some people who are slow are not laggards. The "late majority" often need a little more time for prayer and reflection, or a little more information, before they're ready to embrace a major change. I once led a planning process in which church leaders were increasingly convinced that God was calling them to make a very disruptive change. Near the end of a pivotal meeting, leaders one by one voiced support for the plan. And then Frank spoke up. He wasn't comfortable with the proposed direction yet and didn't want to be rushed on such a major decision. By the next meeting, Frank was in full support despite the disruption that was sure to follow.

It's worth allowing extra time in the change process for people like Frank. Others, however, will ask for more and more and more time. These are the laggards who may be looking for certainty that the new plans will succeed, even though future results are impossible to predict. They have the NASA engineering mindset described in perspective 4. Or they may want to find a solution that won't offend anyone in the congregation, even though someone will always push back when change is proposed.

A different kind of laggard actively works against a proposed change. They're not looking for more time to consider the idea; they are convinced that it is wrong. They may not want to make any changes, or they may have a different solution in mind. Exploring different ideas is an important and healthy part of leading change, but a single objector should not be allowed to hijack the entire process.

And that is the risk of trying to please everyone. Whether the small minority that comprises the rest of "everyone" are people who need far too much time to get to yes or ones who are actively resisting (or some of both), waiting to achieve 100% support for a change often undermines the very change you are hoping to accomplish.

Consider what may be lost if there is a lengthy delay while trying to please everyone. Some of the earliest and most enthusiastic supporters (innovators and early adopters, in Rogers's terminology) may get frustrated and leave. This is particularly ironic since the purpose of delaying is to get everyone on board. It is better to lose a few laggards who are holding out than to frustrate the innovators who can spearhead current and future changes.

Even if those early supporters stay, their enthusiasm may diminish because of the lapse in time or because an innovative proposal has been diluted in an attempt to please everyone. In addition to losing the edge with these supporters, the lost time is a precious resource that cannot be regained. And then there is the energy a leader spends trying to convince holdouts, energy that is then unavailable for other important needs.

Leaders need to have strong support for any significant organizational change. But if you tend to think, "What will it hurt to wait a little longer to get everyone on board?" then take a moment to count the real cost. The art of leading change is knowing when to wait a little longer and when you've waited long enough.

People Pleasers, Charmers, Bulldozers, and Fools

Pastors and ministry leaders who excel in the art of leading change know how to read the people in their organizations so that they can make the tricky decisions on when to press ahead and when to wait. They also know how their own wiring affects their perspective and their internal decision-making.

Many pastors have a deeply rooted tendency to be *people pleasers*. This shouldn't be surprising; vocational ministry is inherently about helping people. It's a small jump from wanting to help people to wanting to please them. And while it's a small jump, this is an important distinction. Jesus did a variety of things to *help* people, but sometimes that meant saying or doing things that didn't *please* everyone, such as healing on the Sabbath or pointing out sin. Is there any doubt about the helpful intent of Jesus's words to the rich young man (Matt 19:16–21)? But "when the young man heard this, he went away sad" (Matt 19:22). Helping people and pleasing them are not the same.

When I teach seminars on change, I often ask the participants for words that they associate with "pastor." The list usually includes things like preacher, teacher, and leader. Sometimes a participant will say something that reveals a good or bad experience, such as mentor or dictator. And without fail, someone will say "shepherd." *Shepherd* is a wonderful, biblical term that should be applied to the role of pastor and other ministry leaders. The danger comes in thinking of a kindly shepherd who gently watches the flock graze in tranquil, green meadows. In reality, shepherds use a firm, steady hand to lead sheep where they won't go on their own.

Completely ignoring or discounting what people think would be scary, and that is not what I'm suggesting. But one of the biggest traps for pastors is the desire to be "liked" by everyone. If people pleasing oozes out of every pore in your body, you will tend to wait for those last few individuals to voice their support. You will probably pull back from a bold decision that will alienate some people in favor of one that is safer and less controversial. While this will protect you from some conflict, and may even be the right instinct at times, be aware of how your natural style of leading may result in missed opportunities.

People pleasers are the personality type that is directly associated with "trying to please everyone," but three other types are important to consider. *Charmers* also tend to please people, but in a very different way. Where people pleasers are constantly trying to find common ground and noncontroversial solutions, charmers have a way of convincing followers of the wisdom of their ideas. They have developed a wealth of skills to accomplish this difficult feat. Charmers are often quite eloquent, combining heart-touching stories, irrefutable logic, and quick answers to demonstrate the soundness of their proposals. They have frequently built tremendous relational capital.

Charmers regularly get their ideas approved, and they have a track record that makes them confident of success even in difficult circumstances. But their very strengths create the real possibility of hollow victories. Because while charm can generate approval, it may not translate into the kind of commitment in which people roll up their sleeves to make the desired changes happen. Some may vote yes and then stand on the sidelines. Some may even abstain from any formal votes (why waste one's breath when the outcome is obvious?) and then participate in some form of underground resistance.

While people pleasers and charmers both work toward very high levels of support for change initiatives, *bulldozers* and *fools* operate at the other end of the spectrum. Bulldozers, once they are convinced of a need for change, press ahead aggressively, even if widespread support is lacking. They rely on the formal authority of their position, a commanding leadership style, a small core team of leaders (often handpicked), and an absolute conviction that they are right. As the name implies, bulldozers ignore or run over people who are slow to get on board, have questions, or disagree. They may have success, at least for a while, but like the charmer, they often lack the broad base of support that is needed for a successful change effort.

Fools also press ahead, but unlike the bulldozers, they have flawed assessments of their own abilities, the depth of support, and the strength of resistance. They overestimate the first two and underestimate the final one. While any of these personalities can ultimately fail in the goal of leading organizational change, the failure of a foolish leader is the most obvious and happens the most quickly.

One long-tenured pastor was highly respected in his denomination. His leadership style, refined and affirmed through years of experience, was a combination of charmer and bulldozer. He was loved by many in his congregation, so the occasional objections to his "do what I say" approach were quickly swept away. He enjoyed mentoring young pastors, telling them that they should take charge and lead like he did. In many cases, however, those pastors had neither the relational capital, natural charm, nor experience to succeed at this game, and they ended up looking like fools.

No one is purely a people pleaser, charmer, bulldozer, or fool, but every leader has a tendency toward one of them. The key is to know your tendencies and to create appropriate counterbalances. The simplest and most effective way to do this is to have a strong leadership team that includes people who know you well, who don't share your same tendencies, and who will offer insights and advice to help you steer a course toward pleasing enough of the right people so that change can flourish.

Who Do You Need to Please?

So if you can't please all the people all the time, who do you need to please? It's an important question, but it can't be answered using a simple formula. The work needed to get this right is like the difference between basic addition and calculus.

Imagine an important decision that requires support from the entire church. "Support" could be a formal vote or just the involvement of the congregation for it to be successful. The decision could be calling a new pastor or launching a capital campaign or changing the Sunday schedule. If 95% of the congregation is in favor of the decision, would that be enough? Would it matter who was among the 5% of nonsupporters? What if it included three of the biggest donors, and the proposal is a capital campaign? Or if all the negative votes were from the choir, and the issue is changing the

Sunday schedule. On the other hand, if the leadership team is unanimously behind a new program but one-third of the congregation is not on board, should you move ahead? Does it make a difference if the leadership team is a group of the pastor's biggest fans versus one that is broadly representative of the congregation?

Before Redemption Church announced the building purchase opportunity to the congregation, the leadership team discussed the level of support needed to move forward. No one thought that a simple majority vote was sufficient, especially since a capital campaign would be required to finance the renovations. They also agreed that a unanimous vote was unrealistic and unnecessary. The team eventually decided that anything less than 80% approval from the congregation would be reason to pull back and reexamine the proposed deal. They believed this threshold was attainable. They also knew setting the bar this high would force them to slow down, listen carefully, and address concerns rather than rushing to vote.

The leadership math of knowing who to please can be complicated, but you can take steps to guide your efforts. The most obvious and important group to consider is the governing or leadership body. No major change can be successfully undertaken without having this group on board. Leaders who press ahead without the strong support of a leadership team will find themselves very far out on a very shaky branch. They may even find someone ready to cut the branch off. Choosing the right people for the leadership team is also important, as discussed in perspectives 4 and 10.

When thinking about the leadership team, "how" is just as important as "who." Specifically, how will decisions be made? This begins with clarity on which decisions need to be made by the leadership team versus ones that can be made by pastors and/or staff or ones that require congregational approval. "How" also calls for understanding the distinction between unanimity and consensus. A unanimous decision, with 100% approval, is wonderful when it is achieved. But creating this expectation for every decision can result in delayed outcomes, pressure on those in the minority, and frustration for those in the majority. Consensus is often not represented by a specific number, but it does imply that the issue has been thoroughly examined and has a high level of support. Most important, however, is for a leadership body to know in advance, not in the heat of the moment, whether it requires unanimity or consensus.

A final step in knowing who to please is simple math. If a major change does not have the support of a solid majority of the congregation, don't try to move forward. I'm not suggesting that all changes should be subject to a congregational vote. I am saying that pushing an agenda without broader support is a risky leadership strategy.

The more difficult part of this question is determining how a congregation is leaning. You don't want to do the hard work of preparing to launch a major change effort only to be blindsided by unexpected resistance from the congregation. If a vote is not required, then how will you know whether they are on board? Ideally, the leadership team is diverse and representative enough to provide an accurate picture of the congregation's likely response. If you're not sure whether the leadership team has a good read, expand the circle of input. This can be done through individual conversations with other people, especially key influencers who are not in leadership roles. It can also be done through meetings with small groups, larger town hall gatherings, or congregational surveys.

Elizabeth, the pastor of Redemption Church, trusted the leadership team, but she also wanted to get a broader sense of how the congregation was reacting to the possible building purchase. So she made a list of twenty key people in the church who were not members of the leadership team and contacted each of them individually. Her goal was to listen to their input on the proposal and answer their questions personally. She thought, "If more than two of these leaders are not supportive after our conversation, it will be a red flag and I'll alert the leadership team that we may have a problem."

Six weeks after the initial announcement of the possible property purchase, the leadership team of Redemption held a meeting to decide whether they were ready to move forward with the congregational vote. The team was still unanimous in their support, but the important question was whether at least 80% of the congregation would vote yes. Three town hall meetings had surfaced a few individuals with deep concerns but no evidence of widespread resistance. Elizabeth reported that her meetings with twenty other key leaders had identified one who was opposed and one who was lukewarm to the idea. In each of those individual meetings, Elizabeth had also asked the leaders what they were hearing from others, and this affirmed the belief that only a handful of people opposed the purchase. By the end of the leadership team meeting, they were ready to schedule the congregational vote, and they were confident that they would far exceed their 80% threshold.

You can't please all the people all the time, but fortunately that is rarely necessary. The wise leader doesn't wait for everyone to get on board but does make sure that enough of the right people are supportive before pressing ahead. That's the art of leading change.

FROM PERSPECTIVE TO PRACTICE

YOU CAN'T PLEASE EVERYONE

- Reflect on your leadership tendencies. Are you more likely to be a people pleaser, charmer, bulldozer, or fool? How can you offset the risks that might be created by your default style?
- Evaluate a current or recent change effort based on the ideas in this perspective. Where did it succeed or fail? What lessons can you learn from this example?

- Work with your leadership team to develop clear guidelines for decision-making. Discuss whether majority, consensus, or unanimity is the criterion for decisions that are made by this team. This is also a good time to clarify which decisions need to come to the leadership team and which ones require congregational approval. How will you make these determinations?

PERSPECTIVE 6

Resisters Are
Not the Enemy

The central tenet of perspective 5 is that you can't please all the people all the time. Even if you have a unanimous vote of approval for a proposed change, some people will be unenthusiastic. They may remain silent or quietly leave. But in many cases, those unhappy people will resist the changes that are being made. Does that make them your enemy?

In many arenas of life, we neatly divide people into two groups: friends and foes. Sports pit one team against another. American politics are defined by two opposing parties. So whenever differences of opinion arise in a church or ministry, our tendency is to identify people as "for us" or "against us" and then label the latter as enemies.

The increased polarization in our society heightens this tendency. Social media and major news outlets allow people to stay in echo chambers that reinforce their views rather than consider different opinions. Attacking people who think differently than we do has become acceptable. While the church should be acting as a positive influence by showing the world how to handle differences, the sad truth is that society is having a much greater influence on the church.

Trinity Church had carefully avoided a "worship war." The church had a vibrant traditional worship service at 11 a.m., so when a contemporary worship service was launched, it was scheduled on Saturday evenings. A few members expressed concerns that the new service would detract from the traditional one, but those complaints died down quickly. For several years, things had gone well, with the traditional service maintaining its strength and the contemporary service growing steadily.

At their annual retreat, the board was asked to reflect on what was working well at Trinity and what needed to change. One leader who attended the contemporary service spoke up: "We love the service, but it's harder and harder for us to get there on Saturday night because of our family's schedule. And we hear the same thing from the friends we invite. I sure wish we could find a way to move the service to Sunday morning."

As the discussion continued, the idea of changing the schedule gained widespread support from the board. A small group was formed to develop a more detailed proposal. They recommended moving the contemporary service to 9:30 a.m. on Sunday and creating a second discipleship hour at 11 a.m. The plan was impressive in its thoughtfulness and detail. After a long discussion and a few revisions, the board unanimously approved the proposal.

The next step was to begin communicating with the church and seeking their input. Not surprisingly, several people had questions about the proposal, and a few had serious objections. A series of meetings with various groups addressed many of these concerns, and three months later the congregational vote was 79% in favor of the change.

If you were Trinity's pastor, how would you react? Knowing that you can't please everyone, is a 79% positive vote enough? Should you press ahead with the change? Were the 21% who voted no strongly opposed, or were they just indicating a personal preference? Will they get on board now that a clear majority have approved the change? And most importantly, what signals does this give you about the road ahead? One thing is certain: thinking of resisters as enemies will draw battle lines that dramatically raise the cost and risks of the change.

The Anatomy of Resistance

Even if a congregational vote is 100% in favor of a change, you should expect some bumps along the road. John Kotter, a leading expert on change, says, "Irrational and political resistance to change never fully dissipates."* Edwin Friedman is even more blunt: "Sabotage is not merely something to be avoided or wished away; instead, it comes with the territory of leading."†

Resistance can take many forms. Some forms are very mild and should not even be thought of as resistance. When a person on the leadership team asks hard questions, that is simply part of the process of thoroughly examining a proposal before making a decision. When a couple asks to meet with the pastor to share their concerns about a plan, this may just be part of a normal process of building understanding and buy-in. Even the person who is among the 21% voting against the schedule change may simply be exercising their rights in a congregational governance system.

So what is resistance? It can take many forms, ranging from mild to inappropriate and destructive. Beyond speaking or voting against a change, some resisters recruit friends to join their opposition. Others may pull away from the church—resigning from volunteer roles, ending financial contributions, or moving their membership. While any resistance is disappointing, these actions are generally seen as normal and within acceptable boundaries.

In more extreme cases, resistance is guided by a political playbook rather than a biblical one. People opposed to a change may share inaccurate or misleading information to influence a decision. Or they may get personal, attacking the pastor and other leaders by questioning their motives or integrity. If the proposed change is

---

* John Kotter, *Leading Change* (Boston: Harvard Business Review, 1996), 132.
† Edwin H. Friedman, *Failure of Nerve: Leadership in the Age of the Quick Fix* (New York: Seabury, 2007), 11.

approved, they may actively undermine the implementation to keep it from succeeding.

As you read these forms of resistance, especially the latter ones, you may feel your gut tightening. Perhaps this has happened to you or to a friend, and you know the hurt it caused. Or you're imagining how painful it would be to experience these kinds of attacks.

In light of these behaviors, how can I maintain that "resisters are not the enemy"? Let me start from a core belief: the people who are resisting change love their church. They are not trying to harm or destroy it. In fact, they often contend that their opposition is based on their belief that the proposed change will hurt the church. They may not be right. Their defense of the status quo may be the real danger. But don't confuse questionable logic with evil motives.

You may think, "Why can't they just get on board? Why don't they see the irrefutable rationale for this change?" But is your case truly irrefutable? When leaders slow down to consider different perspectives, they may find their argument isn't as airtight as they thought it was. Nowhere is this more evident than in the difference between the collective versus personal impacts of a change.

In proposing a change, leaders should be guided by the Spirit to do what will best move the church or ministry toward its vision. The cost of a change may be disproportionately greater for some than others, but a leader should be convinced of the collective benefits before stepping out. It would be wonderful if everyone had the same focus on the collective good, but individual members will often think about a potential change through the lens of "How will this affect me?" To make it more confusing, they rarely acknowledge how much their opinion is influenced by these personal issues but instead wrap their arguments in "What's best for the church" language.

On top of this, when change is in the air, people get anxious. And as experts in human behavior like to say, "Anxiety makes us stupid." No one does their best thinking when they are anxious. As stress rises, people lose their ability to wrestle with all the facets of complex decisions. Instead, their brains shift into "flight or fight" survival mode. If you find yourself wondering why a church member acted so "stupidly" or "irrationally," remember that this is normal behavior in the anxious swirl of change.

Change leaders need to understand what is happening at this individual level, and they also need to consider the broader context. Most churches and ministries do not model healthy conflict. It is healthy to have a meaningful debate about the pros and cons of a potential change. It is normal for some people to disagree with a proposal. Leaders who try to squelch disagreement under the banner of "Let's all just get along" often add fuel to the fire of resistance. If debate can't occur in the open, it doesn't go away; it just goes underground, where resisters will find plenty of unhealthy and unbiblical models for conflict.

The Many Faces of Resistance

It's a mistake to think of disagreement and resistance as synonymous. It's a mistake to treat resisters as the enemy. And it's a mistake to think of all resisters as a homogenous block of people, all with the same perspectives and motivations.

Human beings have a tremendous capacity to fill information gaps with assumptions and stories that portray all resisters as villains. When opposition arises, leaders need to resist the urge to make up generic narratives and simplistic caricatures. Part of the art of leading change is to disaggregate the faceless mass of resisters into individual people, each with a story that is worth hearing. The 21% at Trinity Church who voted against the new schedule illustrate the variety of reasons people resist change and the stories that are easily overlooked.

Megan has been one of the most consistent participants in the Saturday evening service since it was launched. Her two young children are always with her, and her husband comes occasionally. She has often volunteered to help with special events, like the church's annual backpack giveaway, but has never been in a leadership role. None of Trinity's leaders knew of a reason that Megan would vote against the schedule change. But she has been trying to convince her husband to get more involved for years, and his job as a realtor means that he is rarely free on Sunday mornings.

John and Lisa have been in the church for years and have served in a variety of leadership positions. The role they enjoy the most is leading their Bible study class, which they have done for over five years. The class, mostly couples in their forties and fifties, is one of the largest in the church. Surprisingly, several of the people in the class attend the Saturday night service and then come back on Sunday morning just for the class, and others have said that they'd attend the contemporary service if it were on Sunday. But more than half the class loves the traditional worship service, with several being members of the choir. The difference in worship preferences has never been an issue, but the proposed schedule change will force everyone to choose a worship service, which will split the class.

Tim has been a bedrock leader in the children's ministry for years. He teaches the third-grade class on Sunday mornings and twice has stepped up to provide broader leadership after the resignations of children's directors. He has always been concerned that the Saturday evening children's program is weak—"It looks like they sing one song, read a Bible story, and then tell the kids to play and have fun." But he can't wrap his mind around how children's ministry will work with the proposed schedule. After all he's done in the ministry, he's disappointed that he wasn't consulted when the schedule change was being planned.

Julie has been on Trinity's board for two years. She was relatively quiet during her first year, but she eventually found her footing and impressed the rest of the group with her input. She always seemed to think of an important factor that had not occurred to any of the others on the team. When the schedule change was first discussed in the leadership retreat, Julie commented that no other nearby church offered a Saturday evening service. Why should they abandon this unique niche, especially since Trinity's service was still growing? When the board decided to develop a more detailed plan, Julie assumed there would be more opportunity for debate. By the time the subgroup came back with the proposal, it seemed like a done deal. When the board voted on the proposed schedule change, no one noticed that Julie abstained.

The earlier section named a variety of ways—from mild to destructive—that people might resist change. The five people described in this story could engage in any of those forms of resistance. Julie might quietly tell her friends that she didn't really vote for the proposal and encourage them to vote against it. Tim might resign from children's ministry because he felt ignored in the process. John and Lisa might meet with the pastor and say that their entire class is "furious" about the decision and that all are planning to leave the church, statements that are greatly exaggerated. Megan may whisper to her group of friends a rumor that the real motivation for the change is that the pastor's basketball team moved their games to Saturday nights, and he apparently cares more about sports than the church. They might do any of these or other things. Or they might vote against the proposal and then continue to participate and serve as faithful members who are committed to the mission of the church.

The backstories and behaviors of each of these people are different, but there are some common threads that are important to understand. Each has a reason for their opposition. None of them is opposed to the schedule change just because they want to cause problems. In every case, there is more to the story than can be observed on the surface. Even if they resort to less-than-appropriate behavior, as described in the previous paragraph, it does not start from a place of evil intent.

Trinity Church's story also demonstrates a key distinction between resistance to change and unhappiness with the process. Megan, John, and Lisa have specific reasons for objecting to the schedule change. But what about Tim and Julie? Their concerns relate as much to the decision-making process as to the actual proposal. In different ways, each feels the process was rushed and didn't include enough input. Leaders should spend as much time mapping out the *process* for change—how they will seek input and communicate proposals—as they spend on the specific plans for the change. An effective process can greatly reduce resistance.

As you consider the faces of resistance, guard against the possibility of blowing it out of proportion. If you step outside late in the day, your shadow might be twice the length of your body. In the same way, opposition to a change often seems bigger than it really is. Ministry leaders, in particular, are prone to obsessing over a handful of negative comments. Does a single complaint about a sermon drown out the many positive responses? Trinity's 21% negative vote is significant, but the church still had 79% in favor of a major, disruptive shift. In leading change, leaders need to listen to people's concerns, but they must not exaggerate the size of the resistance.

Leaders can and should try to predict the reaction to a proposed change, but they can never be certain how individuals will respond. The individuals from Trinity described in this section might voice their concerns quietly or loudly. They might resist actively or not at all. They might behave in ways that are acceptable or completely out of bounds. Some of their responses will be driven by unseen personal factors or the influence of others around them. As a leader, you can't control the actions of others. But you can choose to see them as individuals rather than as a homogeneous block of "troublemakers." You can also choose how you interact with them, and that can be the real difference maker.

A Pastoral Response to Resistance

What should you do if people who oppose a change are acting like your enemies? Regardless of their stories or their intent, a starting point is to take a cue from Christ's teaching: "But to you who are listening I say: Love your enemies, do good to those who hate you, bless those who curse you, pray for those who mistreat you" (Luke 6:27–28).

It is easy for me to copy and paste these words from an online Bible. It is much more difficult to put them into practice. But consider the alternative. The secular approach to enemies is to keep them at a distance or to go to battle, doing whatever is necessary to beat them. That response almost guarantees a tit-for-tat reaction from the person on the other side of the issue. A small difference of opinion can quickly escalate when leaders put on their battle armor.

Each of the people described in the previous section is opposed to the change in Trinity's schedule. They may cross a line into active resistance, even engaging in actions that are unbiblical. But responding to them in love is the best hope to change their behavior, even if it doesn't change their opinions.

In this context, loving the people who resist change means listening to them and demonstrating care for their concerns. Megan needs an opportunity to describe the pain she feels each time she comes to church without her husband. John and Lisa need to express their anxiety over "losing" their class. Loving resisters means apologizing to Tim for not inviting his input and to Julie for not noticing that she abstained from the board's vote. Sometimes listening to resisters in love will generate solutions. But even when that doesn't happen, a loving response often softens their anger and blunts their attack. It really is true that "a gentle answer turns away wrath" (Prov 15:1).

A leader's responsibility occasionally requires protecting the flock from attacks by genuine enemies. The axiom for this chapter might be restated, "Resisters are *usually* not the enemy." In rare instances, a person may resist change with malicious intent. They may have a vendetta against the pastor or another leader, or they may genuinely want to damage the church. This should never be a leader's first assumption, but if a resister's actions threaten to harm the body, then a firm response is appropriate. This could include removing the person from a position of responsibility or engaging in other forms of church discipline.

Loving and listening to resisters is an important pastoral response, but it should never be the only response. Ministry leaders have a responsibility for the entire flock. For each person at Trinity who voted against the schedule change, almost four people voted for it. Trinity's pastor, and others who are leading change, need to keep their eyes on the vision that God is calling the church to pursue. Leaders may need to say, "I hear your concern and understand your pain, but we still believe this is the right change to make."

Staying focused on the vision is not just about "what we're changing"; it's about "who we're making the changes for." These are often people who do not have a voice, people like Trevor at Trinity Church. He was not among the 21% who voted against the schedule change, nor was he among the 79% who were in favor. That's because Trevor and his two teenage sons stopped coming to Trinity two years earlier. They preferred a contemporary style of worship, but the youth programming was on Sunday mornings. So they dropped out and joined the ranks of people who identify as Christian but don't regularly attend church. Trevor might also be thought of as a resister, but he's resisting the lack of change, and voices like his are rarely heard in the emotion of the decision. (Perspective 9 will look more closely at "who's not in the room.")

The pastoral response is the right way to engage with resistance, and it can make a huge difference in the outcome of the change process, but it is not easy. Resistance hurts; there is no way to avoid this. And dealing with resistance is one of the most difficult parts of a ministry leader's job. It becomes an impossible part of the job if leaders try to face resistance alone and by their own strength.

This is another reason that a strong team and solid spiritual foundation (perspectives 4 and 10) are so important. The weight of resistance—the tension, emotion, and conflict—is simply too much for any one leader to carry. But with the right support and perspective, you may discover that resisters are not your enemies. As that happens, you may also discover that responding to them in love paints a more beautiful picture of the future.

FROM PERSPECTIVE TO PRACTICE

RESISTERS ARE *NOT* THE ENEMY

- What past experiences have you had with resistance? In what ways, positive or negative, has that shaped your current response to resistance?

- Complete this sentence: "When I face opposition, I tend to _____." What about your answer would you like to change in the future?

- Reflect on a current or recent change in which you encountered resistance. Did you make generic assumptions about the people who were resisting, or did you get to know their stories? How might a different approach have affected the outcome?

- What is one action you need to take to respond to opposition in a more pastoral way?

- The burden of dealing with resistance should not be carried alone. Identify one person or a handful of people who can help you shoulder this burden.

AN *Artist's* PERSONAL PERSPECTIVE

The Creative Process

The artistic process, from initial idea to finished creation, is never a straight line. Sometimes, when the public is treated to a peek behind the curtains, we realize just how many twists and turns an artist takes along the way. You might think of the many pencil sketches that were done before the first brushstroke on a masterpiece painting. Or the drafts of lyrics and melodies scribbled onto a sheet of paper and continually refined before a song is recorded. Or the small-scale models that were made before a statue is sculpted. In some cases, often after an artist's death, family members or researchers uncover completely unknown works such as a half-finished song or the manuscript of an unpublished novel.

An efficiency expert might bemoan the "wasted" time represented by all of this "unproductive" meandering. But such an expert's opinion reveals a goal that is different from that of the artist. The efficiency expert is driven by questions of "How much can be produced?" and "How long will it take?" The artist wants to create something of unique beauty. The extra time required for the process is inconsequential if this goal is achieved.

Every doodle on a sketchpad, every random paragraph jotted in a journal is part of the creative process. Sometimes the doodles, paragraphs, sketches, and bars of music will turn into finished products. But even the ones that don't will help the artist visualize what can ultimately be created. These unfinished works are not unproductive detours. An artist experiences them as interesting side streets, not dead ends, knowing the route will eventually take them to a more fulfilling destination.

Leadership in churches and ministries is also a creative process. Leaders need time to "doodle" and "sketch"—to explore different ideas in small, safe settings where they are not subjected to the harsh spotlight of public scrutiny. They need the freedom to test ideas that may not work, knowing that even dead ends can produce learning and growth. And mostly they need the time and space to engage in the deeper, creative, prayerful process that God can use to produce something unique and beautiful.

PERSPECTIVE 7
Momentum Is Your Friend

You've probably seen the cartoons where a tiny snowball is formed at the top of a mountain. With a gentle nudge, it starts down the slope, adding snow with every revolution until it turns into a giant snow boulder. At that point, it is virtually unstoppable.

Every leader wishes for that kind of momentum in their change efforts. And while unstoppable momentum is a myth, there is great power in reaching the point where success begets more success and where people eagerly anticipate what will happen next. If you want to achieve anything close to a bottom-of-the-mountain snow boulder, you need to go back to the top of the mountain to understand how it begins.

Experiments Are Your Friend

If you were at the top of that mountain and knew nothing about snowballs, what would you do? I doubt that you'd try to remember principles from high school physics. Instead, you'd make several attempts to see what worked. You might make snowballs of various sizes, rolling one after another down the slope to observe which one grew most rapidly. Or you'd pack the snow much tighter on some to see if that made a difference. In other words, you'd experiment to learn the best approach.

Experiments, tests, and trial balloons are powerful precursors for momentum in any kind of organization, especially in churches and ministries. Experiments usually cost little and are easy to start. People are less likely to resist an experiment. In fact, many experiments can be done offstage where they are invisible to most of the congregation. An experiment is one of the best ways to take a first step toward a vision, as described in perspective 3.

All these benefits are important, but the greatest value of experiments is the learning they provide. Any experiment that generates new insights should be viewed as a success, regardless of whether it results in the desired outcomes. Learning from one experiment can lead to the next, more effective experiment, which can ultimately lead to something much bigger. The snowball that falls apart gives you clues for how to build one that will stay together.

The mission statement of Lakeshore Church was "Loving people the way Jesus did." The church's leaders had a clear understanding that the "people" in the mission statement included church members and individuals in their community who were not affiliated with the church. For many years, the church's main external expression of its mission focused on ministries that met physical needs.

At a planning retreat, the leadership team had a long conversation about how Jesus loved people. They agreed that Jesus met physical needs, but he was even more concerned about the spiritual needs of the people he encountered. Lindsey, the church's senior pastor, sighed and said, "That is where we are falling way short."

In the discussion that followed, the team considered several ways for the church to become more evangelistic. Their denomination had just created a set of resources to be used in a church-wide evangelism program. But the team didn't think the church was ready. As one leader observed, "We have a lot of people in our congregation who won't even say the E-word." Rather than pushing *evangelism*, they decided to try a different E-word—*experiment*. Members of the leadership team launched two small groups to learn about and practice relational evangelism. Their hope was that these experiments would provide insights on how to raise the evangelistic temperature of the congregation and create firsthand accounts to build momentum for further change.

A trial balloon or experiment can be used for virtually any change that your church is considering. The former allows you to test an idea with a target group, while the latter lets you implement a small-scale version of the idea. If you're considering the addition of a new worship service, a trial balloon could be gathering a core group in someone's living room to assess the need and to dream about what the new worship service should look like. An experiment might be a series of Sunday evening trials before making a big investment in a weekly service.

Experiments may be low cost and relatively easy to conduct, but they are not free in terms of the time or money required. For this reason, experiments should also be purposeful. They should be guided by the church's vision and based on a hypothesis, a simple statement of what the experiment will prove or disprove. The small groups at Lakeshore were being formed to test the hypothesis that typical church members in a small community of mutual encouragement and accountability could learn to engage in relational evangelism. The key phrases in Lakeshore's hypothesis defined the parameters for the experiment. Without a hypothesis, an experiment will often drift aimlessly.

The hypothesis is important, but only if there is also a way to assess results. What is the best metric for Lakeshore's evangelism experiment? You can debate whether it should be the number of participants who are sharing their faith, or the number of people who hear the gospel because of the witness of group members, or the number of people who become Christ-followers. But you wouldn't suggest that the best indicator is the number of participants who give their small group experience a five-star rating. Even though this seems obvious, a lack of clarity about the desired outcome and related metrics is a common factor that keeps churches from building momentum with their experiments.

Sometimes experiments are undermined by an urgency to "do something big now." Beginning a change process with experiments does lengthen the timeline. Lakeshore could expose most of the congregation to the idea of relational evangelism through a church-wide emphasis over the course of a few weeks. But the leadership team recognized that this kind of effort would create a big initial splash with little real impact. The goal for any church should be fruitful ministry, not speed. The insight from experiments should pave the way for that kind of long-term fruitfulness.

Don't Keep It Small

For momentum to be your friend, the experiments in your church need to lead somewhere. Successful experiments can be used to build momentum, but that won't happen by chance. The process for scaling up should be designed as thoughtfully and intentionally as the experiments themselves.

In *Great by Choice*, Jim Collins and Morten Hansen describe the leadership practice of "fire bullets, then cannonballs." They set it up this way: "Picture yourself at sea, a hostile ship bearing down on you. You have a limited amount of gunpowder. You take all your gunpowder and use it to fire a big cannonball. The cannonball flies out over the ocean . . . and misses the target, off by 40 degrees."* Collins and Hansen then explain the better alternative is to fire bullets with small amounts of gunpowder, use the results to calibrate the aim, then accurately fire the cannonball to save the ship.

The kinds of experiments described in the previous section are the bullets. But for a change effort to have any significant impact, leaders will eventually need to move from bullets to cannonballs.

---

* Jim Collins and Morten Hansen, *Great by Choice: Uncertainty, Chaos and Luck—Why Some Thrive Despite Them All* (New York: Random House, 2011), 78.

Sometimes this is done in one big step, like moving from a small home gathering to a new worship service. At other times, several intermediate steps can be taken before firing an organization-wide cannonball.

Lakeshore's leaders knew their church would not become more evangelistic just because a dozen people learned about and practiced relational evangelism in a small group. Lakeshore could have taken learnings from the small groups and launched a church-wide initiative in which every class and small group was asked to use the material on evangelism. Instead, the leadership team decided to do a second round, this time recruiting enough participants for four groups. They recognized that a larger-scale experiment would be a powerful force to convince people who were still hesitant to use the E-word.

An important aspect of scaling up is to incubate change in the early stages. Just as a physical incubator provides the warmth and protection for a baby to grow, the incubation of change means nurturing a new initiative until it can stand on its own. It means identifying the places where resistance could derail the effort. It may require leaders to stay engaged beyond the initial experiment. The more substantial the change, the more incubation is needed.

When Lakeshore's initial small groups end, what is likely to happen if the leaders call everyone together and give an inspiring speech on "making evangelism happen throughout our congregation"? Group members might enjoy a feel-good moment, but the long-term impact will be minimal. Lakeshore will see more success if the small group leaders stay connected with participants, encouraging them to practice what they learned and helping them deal with setbacks. The groups might continue to meet periodically for shared learning and support. This is how change is incubated.

Incubation—just like experimentation—is a means, not the end goal. This may seem obvious, but some leaders are inclined to keep an initiative in this protected space for too long. They may want to maintain control or be anxious that the next step won't go well. It might even be the case that the focus on the small tests (along with many other leadership responsibilities) has left little time to think about how to scale up beyond an experiment.

Scaling up can take many forms. It should be driven by asking, "What is the best way to use the learnings from our experiments or trial balloons to move our church toward the vision?" Lakeshore could continue to use their small-group model, recruiting an ever-growing number of people to experience relational evangelism. Or after the second, larger experiment, Lakeshore could shift to a church-wide emphasis. The best way to scale up is different for each context, but the question of "What's next?" should be on the mind of any leader who wants to make momentum their friend.

Don't Keep It a Secret

When you ask "What's next?" your first thoughts may be about what to *do* next—the steps to take to move from an experiment to a larger endeavor. But it is equally important to think about what to *say* next. Experimentation is typically done with little fanfare. Momentum is built with intentional communication that celebrates wins and demonstrates that change is possible.

The broader question of communication is the subject of perspective 8. This section focuses on how communication contributes to momentum. The key is to be clear about the audience you are addressing and what you want them to do.

Perspective 5 introduced the different categories in Everett Rogers's "diffusion of innovations" theory—innovators, early adopters, early majority, late majority, and laggards. The first two groups are quick to support a change, while the laggards are often actively or passively resisting. But what about the early and late majority? According to Rogers, they comprise 68% of a typical population. They are not the first people to sign up. They often have questions and reservations about the new idea. They are waiting to see if it works. And they are the ones you should target with your momentum-building communication.

Think back to Lakeshore's first two small groups for relational evangelism. Who agrees to participate? It's the innovators and early adopters, the people who are more willing to try something new. People who don't like to say the E-word and who don't think relational evangelism works are not going to sign up for this experiment because it's new and out of their comfort zone. But Lakeshore won't become a more evangelistic church if these hesitant individuals don't get on board.

That is where communication fits in. You may be thinking of a "vision Sunday" or sermon series on "loving people the way Jesus did." This kind of high visibility communication has its place, but it rarely builds enough momentum. If the communication goal is to get reluctant people to take a specific step for the change journey, remember that their default response is "not yet" or "prove it." The most effective message for them is "Look at our success. Don't you want to join our winning team?"

What specific step did Lakeshore's leaders want people to take? Joining one of the relational evangelism small groups. After the first two rounds of experiments, the church was ready to go public with their emphasis. Lindsey did preach a sermon series that focused on the natural, relational ways that Jesus loved people, but this was just one element of the church's communication strategy.

Over the next two years, Lakeshore regularly featured stories about the experiences of small group participants and about people who had come to the church because they had been invited by a neighbor or coworker. They celebrated when the one hundredth person completed the small group experience. These stories appeared in Sunday morning worship services, social media posts, and the monthly newsletter. As Lindsey and her team crafted the message, they were guided by two questions: "What would nudge a reluctant church member to try one of the groups?" and "What will encourage group participants to practice the relational evangelism they've been discussing?'"

The Lakeshore example highlights two important aspects of momentum-building communication. First, rather than telling the congregation what to do, they showed the congregation what is possible because it had already been done. When church members see their friends embracing the desired change, the walls of resistance begin to come down. Second, effective change always requires touching the heart. Statistics on the number of unchurched people in the community may be eye-opening, but the coming-to-faith story of a neighbor is heart-opening. It puts a real face on the statistics and prompts everyone to think about their own neighbors.

Momentum is also built through the simplicity and consistency of the message. Evangelism is a multifaceted subject, but Lakeshore's two guiding questions—how to nudge people to join a group and how to encourage relational evangelism—framed their communication. They returned to the same theme repeatedly for two years.

The simple and consistent approach to communication can help a church avoid the common pitfall of giving equal "airtime" to every program and ministry. While this may seem "fair" and can reduce conflict, it relegates the important message to just a sliver of the overall communication. Another pitfall is a one-and-done campaign mentality in which the new initiative receives focused attention for a few weeks and then vanishes. This is an effective way to introduce a new priority to the congregation, but the communication strategy needs to reflect the reality that change occurs person by person over a longer time.

Lakeshore's communication strategy highlights one other subtle but important message about building momentum. The typical metrics related to evangelism are baptisms or professions of faith, but these are not prominent in Lakeshore's messaging. Why? Because the goal of the church's communication is to get reluctant members to join a small group and to put what they've learned into practice.

Internally, Lindsey and the leadership team tracked baptisms. Based on their initial experiments, they were confident that participation in a group would lead more people to practice relational evangelism, which in turn would result in more baptisms. Effective communication keeps the ultimate goal in mind but may not explicitly focus on that goal.

The message of this chapter is simple: small, successful experiments plus intentional, consistent communication will lead more people to accept and to be enthused about the desired change. And increased acceptance, participation, and enthusiasm will then create more momentum, getting even more people on board. When this happens, momentum becomes your friend.

Momentum Killers

So what could go wrong? Any experienced leader knows that plenty of things can cause the wheels to fall off the bus while driving on the change journey. Even as you're tasting initial success from your experiments, four challenges are important to remember: *distraction*, *overaddition*, *self-promotion*, and *subtraction*.

In the classic leadership book *Good to Great*, Jim Collins describes the power of the flywheel effect.* Enormous energy is needed to start a flywheel moving, and even more energy is needed to increase its speed. But once it is turning at a high rate, the flywheel has tremendous momentum that keeps it rotating on its own for a long time. The mistake of *distraction* occurs when a leader steps away before the flywheel for change has reached its full velocity.

It's easy for pastors and ministry leaders to be distracted, and it's understandable when this happens. Every leader faces daily decisions about where to spend their most precious resource—their time. If things are going well in one area, then they can turn their

---

* Jim Collins, *Good to Great: Why Some Companies Make the Leap and Others Don't* (New York: HarperBusiness, 2001), 164.

attention to a different priority. If the initial experiments—those early turns of the flywheel—are going well, stepping away seems justified: "This experiment doesn't need my focus now." But a flywheel that is deprived of appropriate leadership attention and energy will never gain its full momentum.

Some distractions are inevitable. A major crisis, when it occurs, cannot be ignored. Day-to-day activities—staff meetings, sermon preparation, pastoral care—will continue. Leaders will always have to give time to these "distractions," but they should do so while keeping an eye on the strategic priority that will ultimately transform their church.

Overaddition is a specific kind of distraction that is entirely within a leader's control. It occurs in the pursuit of the next "shiny new thing." Pushing the flywheel around the third or fourth or tenth time is hard work. It may not feel very exciting after the newness has worn off. So some leaders step away in search of something different to spend time on. This mistake can kill momentum more quickly than any of the others. Not only is the existing priority deprived of a leader's attention, but focusing on the shiny new thing will often distract other people.

As you communicate successes to build momentum, what pronoun do you use most often? First-person singular pronouns ("I" and "me") will be heard as *self-promotion*, whereas first-person plural ones ("we" and "us") convey team effort. Regardless of how much of the work you have done to get to this point, you can't realize the vision without the contributions of others. And you certainly can't get there without God. If you want to keep building the momentum of the flywheel, every small and large victory should be celebrated as a "we"—giving credit to God and the faithful people who labored alongside you.

Subtraction is a different kind of momentum killer. One of the most difficult aspects of leading change is the loss that people feel or experience and the opposition that results from this loss. When a program or ministry is eliminated to make room for something different, resistance to the new one will rise. People may already be reluctant to embrace relational evangelism at Lakeshore, but if funding is redirected from a community assistance ministry to support the new evangelism emphasis, reluctance will turn into resistance.

Some subtraction, and the loss that comes with it, is inevitable. The art of leading change is to prevent that loss from turning into momentum-killing resistance. Subtraction that occurs gradually or by attrition is often better than a sudden switch. When a quicker change is necessary, a pastoral response to the people who are experiencing loss can soften their pain and lessen their resistance.

That small snowball at the top of the mountain can turn into a powerful, giant snow boulder. But it does so one snowflake at a time, just as momentum is built in your church one person at a time. Momentum isn't an abstract concept or a principle in a physics book. It's a human dynamic that can propel your change journey forward.

FROM PERSPECTIVE TO PRACTICE

MOMENTUM IS YOUR FRIEND

- What significant change is needed in your church or ministry? What experiment can you design related to that change?
- What criteria will you use to evaluate the success of your experiment? Be as specific as possible.
- If your experiment works as planned, what will the next step be? How do you envision scaling up?
- Design a communication plan that will build momentum for your desired change. Invite other leaders to review and give input on the plan.
- Which of the four momentum killers—distraction, overaddition, self-promotion, or subtraction—is most likely to be a problem for you?

PERSPECTIVE 8

What They Heard, Not What You Said

"**P**astor, I sure wish I had known sooner about tonight's meeting. I already have plans, so I can't be there. But we just don't think you should be giving away that much money when the church has so many needs."

Several different thoughts and emotions swirl in your head as you try to decide how to respond in this brief interaction with a church member. The meeting has been publicized in every possible way for over a month, so you're tempted to say, "If you'd just pay attention!" The proposed change was initiated by the elders, so you want to defend yourself and say, "It wasn't my idea. *I'm* not giving away any money." Of course, you were thankful when the elders made the recommendation because the church has had a history of giving lip service to external needs while directing most of its resources internally. It crosses your mind to say, "It's about time to think of someone other than ourselves." And then there's the ominous "we" in her statement—is there an active campaign to oppose the plan? You think about saying, "You know that gossip is a sin."

Jacob, the senior pastor at Memorial Avenue Church, had a split second to decide what he would say. Earlier in his career, he might have blurted out any of these things, and he would have paid a high price. As an experienced pastor, however, he sighed and simply said, "I'm sorry you didn't know, Ms. Thompson. We tried to get the word out. If you have concerns, please send me an email."

Every pastor and ministry leader has stories like this. Effective communication can make or break a change process. But no matter how hard you try, it doesn't seem to be enough. You'll never reach the point where everyone reads and retains everything the church communicates, just like you'll never have 100% support for a change. If the message isn't getting through, it's not enough to insist "We've done our best." You may be surprised at what you'll learn by asking what is being heard rather than focusing on what has been said.

Ms. Thompson obviously missed the notices about the meeting, but what did she hear about the proposed change? Jacob thought the message was straightforward. The church plans to shift its budget so that 50% of contributions will be given away for missions. This shift will occur over five years as debt is paid down and as the church grows. It is a big change, one that will surely be met with some concerns, but the core message is simple. How could it be misunderstood?

Ms. Thompson had glanced at the earlier article that explained the elders' recommendation for a "50-50 budget," so she understood the proposal to allocate half of the church's income for missions. But she overlooked the fact that the change was to be made over several years as debt was paid down. She assumed staff and programming would be cut, and she was particularly concerned that the women's ministry director might lose her job. One of Ms. Thompson's friends had heard that half of the money raised in the recent capital campaign would be redirected for missions rather than for building renovation and debt reduction as originally advertised. These two friends shared their concerns with the other women in their Bible study group, and all agreed "We can't let 'them' do this to our church."

Even with the best communication, scenarios like this may occur. But the absence of effective communication greatly increases the chances of your plans for change being derailed. Whether it's preventing a small misunderstanding from becoming an out-of-control rumor or creating the excitement to rally a congregation behind a new initiative, a well-designed communication strategy is a vital part of any change effort.

The Ripples of Communication

You're standing on the shore of a lake and throw a rock far out into the water. As the waves ripple out from the center, you watch to see if they'll reach all the way to the shore. Imagine that scene for a moment.

What factors make it more or less likely the ripples will travel all the way to the shore? Size is one factor—a large rock will produce much bigger ripples than a small pebble. Distance also matters—the farther you throw the rock, the less likely the ripples will be to reach the shore. If it's a tranquil day with no other waves, the movement of the ripples will be easier to follow even as they grow smaller.

This analogy highlights many of the challenges of communication in church and ministry settings. Consider the factors in reverse order. Instead of a tranquil day, what would you see in the ripple pattern on a windy day? Add to that a few motorboats racing around on the lake. You'd barely see the ripples at the point of impact, much less near the shore. In a similar way, church communications never occur in a vacuum. The people receiving your communications are constantly bombarded with other messages and distractions. Even when you think you're communicating to a "captive audience"—such as when making announcements in a worship service—remember that two-thirds of the congregation are not in the building, and the ones in attendance may be checking their phones or making a mental to-do list in that moment.

What about distance? The leadership team and staff are closest to the center. They have generally been part of the discussions, so they are already well informed. Even in cases where they were not at the table, they know key decisions affect them, so they pay closer attention. The next ring are other leaders and the most active members. They are farther from the center and don't pay attention to every communication, but they tend to stay well informed. As you continue to move farther out to the average members and then to those who are nominally involved, you'll find less and less communication getting through.

Finally, the prominence or "size" of the communication matters, just like the size of the rock. If you want to increase the likelihood that the people who are farther from the center will hear a message, give it the weight it needs. Make it the headline in your weekly news or the subject of a special communication that is completely separate from the normal routine. Use the pastor or board chair for the handful of messages that really matter. If one large rock isn't enough to create the ripples you want, you don't have to give up. Repeatedly throwing rocks into the same spot in the lake will magnify the impact. In the same way, thoughtful and creative repetition of key messages about change is an important way to get the word out to the people who are farthest from the center.

Unfortunately, church communications tend to look like the person who throws a lot of rocks into the lake, all landing at different places. Rather than a clear set of ripples spreading from one central point, the water will become a mess of unsynchronized waves that cancel one another out. In churches, the sheer volume of messages, not to mention the overuse of "This is really important," can become an impediment to effective change. Meaningful change is not possible without meaningful communication.

Developing a Communication Strategy

You wouldn't even consider launching a major change without developing a plan for how it will be implemented. In the same way, you need to develop a plan for how the change will be communicated.

One of the core principles with any communication is "Know your audience." When change is on the horizon, leaders need to define who will be affected and build their communication strategy around those people. Sometimes a change will clearly impact a segment of a congregation, such as new programming for children's ministry. Sometimes a change is big enough that the entire congregation needs to know, such as a change in the Sunday schedule.

What about the budget at Memorial Avenue Church? Since no cuts are being made to staff and programming, Jacob thought most members would have little reaction. He overlooked the ownership that members feel around church finances and the possibility that the plan could be misunderstood.

"Knowing your audience" is more than identifying the target groups; it is also understanding what is important to them. Ms. Thompson was concerned about possible cuts in the women's ministry, but another member will be concerned about reductions in the youth ministry. You won't be able to address every individual concern in the broad communications, but you should find the common themes that are important. For Memorial Avenue, an important common theme is the impact of the proposal on existing ministries and staff.

To stay one step ahead of congregational concerns, leaders can create a list of answers to frequently asked questions (FAQs). The process of creating the list can be every bit as valuable as the information in the list. How does a leader know the FAQs? Start by asking the leadership team for input, but don't stop there. This is a great opportunity to pause and think about concerns that are likely to arise or to go out and take the congregation's pulse.

Responding to concerns, whether in FAQs or town halls or individual meetings, is important, but it is also one of the places where leaders can get in trouble. The process of responding to people's questions is intended to address concerns and generate support for a proposed change. But what happens if a leader knows the answer to a particular question won't be popular? Far too often in these moments, leaders give answers that are vague and ambiguous, or they backtrack slightly from the plans so that the questioner will walk away happy.

To Jacob's surprise, Ms. Thompson rearranged her schedule and came to the town hall meeting. As she thought about the proposal, her concern shifted from the longer-term question about the women's ministry director to the budget for the coming year. The women's ministry had requested a significant increase in their program funding to pay for childcare for two new Bible studies. When it was her turn to speak, Ms. Thompson asked, "Will women's ministry still be able to get the additional funds that we were promised for next year?" Jacob paused, then answered, "Women's ministry is such an important part of the life of our church. We're going to do our best to support the new plans that you all have worked so hard on."

What just happened? Jacob thought he gave a wise answer, one that satisfied Ms. Thompson without making any firm commitments. But remember, it's what they hear, not what you say. And Ms. Thompson heard support for the funding increase. Meanwhile, the finance chair's stomach was in knots, knowing that the requested increase had been cut from the preliminary budget. Jacob's answer may have avoided disappointment today, but it created future conflict, one in which an exasperated Ms. Thompson will angrily insist, "But you said . . ."

Anticipating and dealing with objections are a necessary part of the communication strategy for any change, but the positive, forward-looking element is more important. Perspective 3 describes the necessity of a compelling vision in the change process. The vision should be the driver for any significant change in a church or ministry. But don't leave it to the people to make the connection between the vision and the specific change. Connect the dots for them. Be explicit about how a specific change relates to the broader vision.

Memorial Avenue's proposal to devote 50% of giving for missions was not a random idea from an elder who thought they were spending too much on salaries and internal programming. The church's vision emphasizes the importance of turning outward and being Christ's presence in their community and the world. The funding shift was just one of several changes to move the church toward this vision. In developing the communication strategy for the budget proposal, church leaders needed to remind the congregation of the direction set by the vision.

Of course, a critic may say, "When we approved the vision two years ago, I didn't know that we'd make such a radical shift in our budget." Remember, it's what they heard. At the time of the vision rollout, Jacob and the leadership team briefly mentioned that the new vision would have big implications for the budget, but they didn't offer any details. In fact, the elders did not settle on the 50-50 idea until a year after the vision was adopted. Change is an ongoing process, and so is the communication to support change.

The communication strategy should reflect the variety of people in the congregation. This includes the different factors that concern and inspire them and the types of messages that speak most clearly to them. Some people respond best to messages that target the head, while others are most influenced by messages aimed at the heart. One focuses on the hard facts that can be conveyed with tables and graphs. The other needs to see pictures and hear narratives of individuals whose lives have been touched. People who prefer head-oriented communication are wary of "soft," anecdotal information, while the other side sees the hard data as impersonal and often confusing. But it's not an either-or choice. Communicating for effective change incorporates both.

The 50-50 budget proposal for Memorial Avenue lends itself to hard data. Financially savvy elders can create large slide decks showing the numbers in detail, including multiyear projections of how the church can make the shift without hurting programs. Their presentation will be impressive to other like-minded people in the congregation and may convince a number of fact-oriented skeptics.

But if widespread congregational support is the goal, the communication strategy should also touch people's hearts with images and stories from the mission partners that will benefit from the increased funding.

You may be thinking, "I don't have this kind of time. Is developing a thorough communication strategy really that important?" The short answer is a resounding "Yes!" Because if you don't spend the time to plan your communications, you'll spend more time dealing with the consequences of communication failures.

New inventions are created every year, but many of them never get to the market, even some with superior features. The inventors may be geniuses in product design, but they'll only be successful if they are also savvy marketers. Just like the marketing plan for a new invention, your communication strategy is critical for the success of your change efforts.

Relay Stations and Listening Posts

At this point, you may feel a little uneasy. Developing a comprehensive communication strategy that is effective with the many different groups in your church or ministry sounds overwhelming. But the good news is, you don't have to do it alone, and you don't have to determine all the details in advance.

Methods of communication have changed over the course of human history. Until the last two decades, communicators have always recognized that they are dependent on others to get their messages out. Whether the mode of communication was smoke signals, Pony Express, telegraph, or print newspaper, multiple people touched, and sometimes shaped, the information.

The internet has fundamentally changed the nature of communication, but access to information and ease of pushing messages out do not automatically translate into effectiveness. People only absorb a fraction of the communication in church-wide emails, letters, videos, and announcements, no matter how well crafted these are. The distance from the center to the outer rings is just too great. Because what they heard is what matters, change leaders need to relearn lessons from those earlier eras.

The common denominator of those older forms of communication is their reliance on the people in the middle. The same is true when major changes need to be communicated for a church or ministry. In this case, the people in the middle are the influencers and leaders of existing groups—classes, small groups, the choir, and volunteer teams for a specific ministry or mission. Within these groups, the relational distance is much less, and communication is stickier.

If a message needs to be widely heard and understood, don't shy away from using people in the middle as essential relay stations. In this form of communication, the message is only as effective as the messenger, so invest time to make sure these intermediate communicators understand their assignments and the key points to be conveyed. The more that they are up to speed, the less distortion there will be when the message reaches its final destination.

These relay stations serve a powerful two-way purpose. Not only can they distribute important messages; they can act as listening posts to bring information back to the leadership team. Anyone serving as a messenger to communicate outwardly to segments of the congregation should also be a conduit for feedback. This isn't complicated; they simply need to allow time for questions and input after delivering a message. Then they need to distill what they heard and pass it back to the leadership team.

As simple as this sounds, it is often overlooked. Some leadership teams believe they are representative of the congregation and therefore are unlikely to learn anything new. Other leadership teams are arrogant. They become convinced that they've spent more time looking at the issue and are smarter than the congregation, and therefore any feedback will be unhelpful or irrelevant. Even if they're not arrogant, a leadership team may not want to hear feedback because they don't want to take the time to adjust their plans. Wise leadership teams, however, create intentional ways to listen to the congregation when major changes are being proposed.

A final factor that can prevent the two-way flow of information is the way pastors view their roles. Vocational ministry places more emphasis on outward communication than virtually any other profession. Pastors are trained to "tell" more than to listen, so the reflex to be attuned to important feedback simply doesn't come naturally.

These factors may explain why leaders don't avail themselves of listening posts, but they shouldn't be treated as valid excuses for one-way communication. Feedback from the congregation may lead to refinements that make a proposed change even better. But even more important, feedback provides insights into what people are hearing. It doesn't matter what you're saying if you don't know what they are hearing. If you don't know what they're hearing and how they're reacting, you won't know how to respond to resistance or adjust your communication.

In contrast, awareness of what people are hearing is a tremendous benefit in leading change. Simple misunderstandings can be corrected. Information gaps can be filled. Major divides can be bridged with creative solutions. But this only happens when leaders quit focusing on what they said and start asking what is being heard.

What would have happened if Jacob had been aware of the storm brewing in Ms. Thompson's Bible study? A meeting with the leaders of the group might have answered their concerns, thereby avoiding an ambush at the town hall meeting and the subsequent fallout. Not only that, but increased awareness could highlight other flaws in the communication of the budget proposal that might have been addressed proactively.

Communications for a major change initiative will never be perfect. No matter how often you avoid a messy scenario like the one with Ms. Thompson, you will still have surprises and stumbles. But if you don't shift your mindset to focus on what is being heard, you'll always be shooting in the dark. And that's a risky and unnecessary strategy when leading change effectively is vital for your future.

FROM PERSPECTIVE TO PRACTICE

WHAT THEY HEARD, NOT WHAT YOU SAID

- Reflect on a recent situation when communication did not go as intended. What went wrong? What could have been done better?
- Identify an upcoming initiative and create a small team to develop a comprehensive communication strategy. The initiative should be important enough to justify this effort. Be clear about the target audience and what they care about. Evaluate the effectiveness after the plan has been implemented.
- For important moments, do you receive enough two-way communication to assess whether your message is being heard? If not, what steps should you take to open the lines for information to flow back to you and the leadership team?

AN *Artist's* PERSPECTIVE

The Power of Perception

A visual artist's eyesight may not be any better than that of other people, but their perceptive ability is much more refined. According to Betty Edwards, the average person's brain "doesn't want too much information about things it perceives—just enough to recognize and to categorize. . . . Because the brain is overloaded most of the time with incoming information, it seems one of its functions is to screen out a large proportion of incoming perceptions."* Edwards's words are written for artists in training, but they apply just as readily to leaders in training.

If you go to the park to meet a friend for a picnic, you may notice other people, their pets, the trees, and the clouds in the sky. But after a few minutes, you probably couldn't describe any of these in detail. An artist who is painting the picnic scene will take it all in. She will observe the shape of the picnic basket, the colors of the blanket, the angle at which you and your friend are reclining, and the relative size of the distant grove of trees. This information is readily available to any observer, but most people pay little attention to these details. The artist, on the other hand, knows that accurate perception is essential for the success of her work.

Is perceptive ability a natural-born trait? Maybe to a degree. But the better explanation is that successful artists have learned to slow down and observe. Edwards offers an "upside-down drawing"

---

* Edwards, *Drawing on the Right Side*, 76–77.

exercise to illustrate this point. Students are asked to take a picture, such as a portrait of a person, and turn it upside down. They then try to re-create their own drawing starting at the top (which is the bottom of the original picture) and working their way down. According to Edwards, the more accurate drawings are produced by the students using the upside-down picture than by the ones looking at the image turned the right way.[*] Rotating the picture 180 degrees forces the brain to slow down and perceive differently.

Leaders need heightened perception. They need to understand the readiness for change within their church or ministry and the likelihood of opposition. They need to gauge whether trust is high or low. Just like the artist, leaders must pay full attention to everything in their environment, both big and little. Even though many leadership settings seem to demand a frantic pace, slowing down and perceiving more fully are vital for leading change. Without accurate perception, important leadership decisions can go awry because of missed details.

---

[*] Edwards, 52–54.

Who Is *Not* in the Room?

Throughout this book, we've seen that the art of leading change is all about people—earning their trust, helping them understand and get excited about a vision, listening to their concerns, finding the right leaders for new initiatives. But the previous chapters have not focused on a particularly important group of people—those who are on the outside.

Dietrich Bonhoeffer said, "The church is the church only when it exists for others."* Jesus clearly focused on outsiders during his time on earth. In a society that shunned those who were "less than," Jesus demonstrated love for women, people with physical disabilities, and other outcasts. He cared for people who were ethnic and religious outsiders, such as the Roman centurion and the Samaritan woman at the well. In the parable of the great banquet, Jesus portrays the host saying, "Go out quickly into the streets and alleys of the town and bring in the poor, the crippled, the blind and the lame" (Luke 14:21).

Church leaders rarely argue with the notion that the gospel is for all people and that we are called to demonstrate Christ's love toward people who are not like us. But when faced with specific decisions, the tendency of most churches is to focus on the desires and preferences of the people who are in the room, not the outsiders. The unspoken message is "All are welcome, as long as they come on our terms."

---

* Dietrich Bonhoeffer, *Letters and Papers from Prison* (New York: Touchstone, 1997), 382.

Welcome to the "Club"

Reggie McNeal says the North American church is often like "a clubhouse where religious people hang out with other people who think, dress, behave, vote, and believe like them."* This condemnation may seem too harsh, but reflect for a second on how a club functions and the ways your church may resemble one. Clubs have formal processes for becoming a member, steps generally intended to make sure the right people get in and to exclude the wrong people. The "right" people are ones who are similar to the others in the club. If someone wants to join the club, they know they need to change enough to fit in.

I am not saying we shouldn't care what church members believe. Core Christian beliefs are important. But consider all the other barriers that stand in the way for outsiders who want to explore what it means to follow Jesus. Our church language is full of terms that are known only by insiders. Worship services may have songs or traditions that are incomprehensible to a newcomer. Relationships that have existed for years can signal that a group is closed, regardless of their superficial words of welcome. Someone who dresses differently than the norm is sure to get more than one questioning glance.

The board of St. Matthew's Church scheduled an all-day meeting to revisit the church's vision and to plan for the future. Rather than meeting on their campus, they arranged to gather at another local church that had a reputation for reaching young adults. When the board arrived, they were greeted by a young man who took them to their meeting room. As he showed them around, he told them he was a local visual artist who had been a nonbeliever. He had come to the church looking for hope and a fresh start during a difficult time in his life.

---

* Reggie McNeal, *The Present Future: Six Tough Questions for the Church* (San Francisco: Jossey-Bass, 2003), xvi.

Later that day, St. Matthew's board began discussing how they wanted their church to reach people like the young artist they had met. One board member, Candace, challenged the others: "Do we really mean that? Would someone who is covered in tattoos and piercings be made to feel welcome if they came to St. Matthew's tomorrow?" Other board members pushed back, arguing that their congregation was very friendly and that all people would be welcome. But Candace stood firm: "Half the men in our congregation wear a coat and tie on Sundays. The people who are dressed 'casually' could be on the cover of a fashion magazine. My adult son, Aaron, looks more like the guy we met earlier today. He said he wouldn't come back to our church after all the looks he got the last time he was there."

Physical appearances are an easy example of the club mentality, but the issue is much deeper and more pervasive than this. The central question is not "How can we do a better job of welcoming people who are different?" That question implies assimilation—being more tolerant of people who look different with the expectation that they will become more like the other members over time. The real question is "How much are we—the insiders—willing to change to live into our church's gospel vision?"

Animating the Vision

A church's vision statement almost always makes room for outsiders—sort of. The specific language may talk about loving "others" or "neighbors" or "all people" or "the world." It may proclaim the importance of sharing God's love or the gospel. All these phrases are externally oriented. They seem to say that outsiders matter.

So where does the breakdown occur? We have already looked at the importance of having a vision and taking the right next step toward that vision (perspective 3). The vision is important, but those simple, externally oriented words need to be animated to bring the vision to life.

The natural human tendency is to focus on self and to choose the path that is most familiar and comfortable. Left on their own, people can easily interpret those common vision phrases in the ways that are least disruptive. "Loving neighbors" can be interpreted as loving the people who are already in our church community or ones who act and think like us. Or church members may decide the best way to "love the world" is to give money to international missions rather than rolling up their sleeves to partner in missions with local entities.

To combat this tendency, leaders need to regularly remind people of the vision *and its interpretation*. The stories we tell, the victories we celebrate, and the metrics we track will all help the congregation understand what the vision really means. Think of them as clues that can point outward or inward. Some people may need a lot of clues before it sinks in that the neighbors whom they are called to love may look very different, just as in the case of Jesus's parable of the good Samaritan.

My church's vision statement includes the phrase "loving others," with an explanation that we commit to "privilege the unbeliever." Each Sunday, a prayer is offered by a different layperson as part of the worship service. The week before the service, the person who will be praying receives instructions to "remember unbelievers are listening" and "make our language accessible, being careful to avoid Christian subculture jargon." In his sermons, our senior pastor often says this is a place for people who are exploring Christianity or who have doubts about faith. Does this mean the people in our church think of outsiders first? Not always. We're far from perfect, but I believe we are a little more attuned to outsiders and a little less insular because of these reminders.

A great visual artist has a unique ability to make a painting or sculpture seem almost alive. Think of the ceiling of the Sistine Chapel or the statue of David, both masterpieces by Michelangelo. A great musician can evoke deep feelings through their arrangement of simple notes and words. In the same way, a leader's job is to animate the vision, helping people see far more than the words on a page.

Nowhere is this truer than with the vision's implications for outsiders. Is your congregation's vision intended to be a picture of God's preferred future, one in which outsiders are genuinely loved and accepted? Then the vision needs to be animated and infused with meaning. Each time you remind the congregation of the full meaning of the vision—through explanations and challenges and stories—the picture becomes more vibrant and room is created for outsiders.

Seeing the Outsider

The leader of a Christian nonprofit once told me, somewhat cynically, "It's easy to raise money for starving children in Africa." He was describing the strong emotional pull we experience when we see a picture of a child who has desperate physical needs.

This raises an important question for church leaders: shouldn't the outsiders who are part of your vision have a name and face? The people who are not currently in the room need to become real for an externally oriented vision to have real power. Their stories and hurts and hopes will be much more effective at turning your congregation outward than a set of statistics.

The board of St. Matthew's Church got a glimpse that made the outsider much more tangible than a generic image of "young adults" or the "arts community." Candace was already keenly aware because her son was one of those outsiders. Her willingness to share her story and her pain changed the tone and direction of the board retreat. More than once as they discussed new ideas, board members asked Candace, "How do you think Aaron would respond?"

There is power and danger in this example. Aaron and the young artist who greeted the board are easily distinguished from the people who normally attend St. Matthew's. The visible differences are striking. This can be the case with many kinds of outsiders. Differences in age or skin color or clothing are just some of the clues that immediately signal someone is not an insider.

But a person can be an outsider even if they appear to be just like insider church members. A single parent wonders if she has a place in a church where everyone seems to be married. A college dropout worries about fitting into a church full of longtime Christians who talk in lofty theological language. A person who walked away from faith after middle school doubts that someone with questions about Christianity and a superficial knowledge of the Bible will really be welcome.

In each of these cases, the person is an outsider, but the factors that make them an outsider are mostly invisible. In fact, the differences are completely invisible from a distance. But for the outsider, those differences are readily apparent and can be sources of anxiety as they wonder how well they fit in a specific church.

Imagine the college dropout's first visit to St. Matthew's. He's wearing his only sports coat in order to look like everyone else. After the worship service, a member greets him warmly. In the conversation that follows, the visitor asks, "What's this church like?" He's really wondering, "Is there room here for someone like me?" The friendly church member eagerly replies, "We're theologically orthodox in the broad Calvinistic tradition, but with a less rigid view on election." How will the visitor respond? He will probably be confused and conclude that someone like him will not fit in. The saddest thing about this vignette is that the church member is clueless about how her comment landed with the visitor. She's proud of the church's theology and thought her answer was wonderful.

This story may be an exaggeration, but only slightly. It underscores how easily outsiders can be pushed away, especially when the differences are less visible. To overcome the tendency to miss the mark, churches that are serious about the outsider need to see them in 3D. Their stories need to be understood. They need to have individual names and faces, not just labels such as "skeptic" or "millennial" or "urban."

Consider the young artist who first greeted the board of St. Matthew's. The two-minute version of his story created more interest and awareness than if the board had just walked past him in the entrance, but their knowledge is still only an inch deep. They don't even remember his name, and they've only heard a fraction of his story. In contrast, several of the board members have known Aaron since he was a child, and they all know about him through Candace. If Candace had not been a board member, a conversation that started with good intentions ("How can we reach people like that unbelieving artist?") would probably have lost energy or arrived at mistaken conclusions.

It is not easy for a church to become more concerned about outsiders than insiders, but there's a ray of hope in this specific challenge. Once an insider has truly begun to know an outsider and to see them as God sees them, it is difficult to unsee them. And once that happens, the insider becomes more sensitive to the language and practices that can make an outsider feel unwelcome and unwanted. So how can a church begin to become more aware of the needs and concerns of the people who are not in the room?

Making Room for Outsiders

The process of becoming more sensitive to outsiders, as with most other changes in a church, must begin with the leadership team. They have the respect of the congregation, so their words and behaviors carry disproportionate weight. They also have responsibility for any strategic shifts that need to be initiated. And they will feel the heat from insiders who are unhappy with changes that make the church more outward facing.

But how do you move the needle within a leadership team? One way is to return frequently to the vision and to its interpretation as described earlier in this chapter. Another solution is to create specific opportunities for the team to learn about or interact with outsiders. Even more effective is to place people on the leadership team whose lives regularly intersect with outsiders.

Some potential leaders are deep insiders; they have been part of the church for years and have little meaningful contact with people on the outside. Others who are equally qualified for leadership may be much closer or more attuned to outsiders. These potential leaders may be like Candace, whose son typifies the people St. Matthew's would like to reach. Other examples might include a church member who is a teacher in the neighborhood elementary school, a former outsider who is now actively involved in the church, or a member of the welcoming team who has demonstrated an ability to connect with all kinds of visitors. The leadership team doesn't have to be composed entirely of people with this kind of heightened sensitivity to outsiders. A handful can be enough to raise questions about whether decisions are being made with an eye toward who is not in the room.

These solutions point toward a broader goal: any strategic decision should be run through the filter of how it will impact the outsiders who are an integral part of the church's vision. A proposal that keeps them at arm's length or pushes them away needs to be revisited.

Prior to their all-day meeting, the St. Matthew's board had been on the verge of starting a new Sunday morning worship service designed to attract young adults. After Candace challenged them, they realized that people like Aaron were unlikely to come to this worship service. Regardless of the style and feel of the actual service, it would be impossible for a visitor to make it into the building without encountering a host of well-dressed insiders. Rather than trying to change the entire congregational ethos on Sunday mornings, the board decided that the right next step would be to start the new worship service on Sunday evenings when the facility was not being used and when they could create an entirely different vibe.

The primary leadership team is the right starting point for asking who is not in the room, but the question needs to be expanded to other leaders in the church. The leadership team can make the strategic decisions to privilege outsiders, but it is the day-to-day decisions and actions of other leaders that can embody an outward-oriented culture. Three groups, in particular, are vital for this shift: leaders of small groups and Bible study classes, children's ministry volunteers, and the welcome or hospitality team. Each can play central roles in genuinely welcoming outsiders and beginning to shift the culture for the entire congregation.

Sometimes the loneliest place to be is in the middle of a crowd. Outsiders—those who perceive they are different from a church's members—will pay close attention to the clues in the larger gathering about whether they fit, but their real question is whether they will be accepted in a smaller relational network. That is why small groups and Bible study classes are so important. The leader of the group or class sets the tone. There is a world of difference between a warm welcome and a superficial greeting, and between an attitude of genuine acceptance versus one of lukewarm tolerance. This tone communicates volumes to the outsider and sends an important signal to insiders. Leaders can also guard against the Christian lingo that implies "This is a members-only club," which is a common barrier in some groups and classes.

The tone of genuine acceptance is even more important in children's ministry. Adults will endure a certain amount of coolness or distancing, knowing that it takes time to break into a new group. But no one wants to subject their children to being treated as "others." The condescending glance from a children's ministry volunteer or a child's after-class story of being embarrassed is all it will take for an outsider parent to give up on a church.

"You only get one chance to make a first impression." This may be an overused cliché, but it is true, especially for the experiences that outsiders have when they visit a church for the first time. The team of people who welcome guests—greeters, ushers, parking lot attendants, information desk staff—are the primary creators of first impressions. You might hope that these roles are always filled with the warmest, most engaging, and most visitor-sensitive volunteers. Unfortunately, that is not the case in some churches where hospitality volunteers preferentially welcome their insider friends. On the other hand, one greeter who takes a genuine interest in an outsider and goes the extra mile to make them feel accepted can create a lasting impression.

If you and your church are serious about making room for outsiders, be intentional about how these three groups of volunteers are trained. The same awareness-raising steps that are applicable for a leadership team can be adapted for each group. If these insiders become outsider sensitive, they can form a critical mass that influences the rest of the congregation. What if the usher who was known for wearing a suit and a frown started showing up in a polo shirt and offering his warmest greetings to people he didn't know? Maybe this is just a dream, but imagine how many members would take note of the change.

The question of who is not in the room is one of the most difficult for a church to ask. It is difficult because of the very fact that we're asking about people who are not visible. It is much easier to think about the people we see and hear and know—the people who are in the room. That is why a theme running through this chapter is to find ways to make these invisible people more real.

The other difficulty with asking "who is not in the room" goes to the heart of change resistance, particularly in churches. Even Christians with the best intentions allow self-interest to seep into their decisions. It is just part of our fallen, human nature to care more about insiders—ourselves and those closest to us—than outsiders. Putting others ahead of self is central to the gospel message and also incredibly difficult to do consistently. That is why, as we'll see in the next perspective, we can't really care for the people who are not in the room unless the Holy Spirit is working on the stuff that is inside of us.

FROM PERSPECTIVE TO PRACTICE

WHO IS *NOT* IN THE ROOM?

- Plan the agenda for your next leadership team meeting. Identify a specific topic or decision where it would be appropriate to ask who is not in the room. Use this question as a springboard for a deeper discussion about the outsiders your church hopes to reach.
- With your leadership team, create a three-dimensional picture of your church's outsider(s). Identify some specific, known individuals if possible. What do these outsiders look like? What do they believe? What questions are they asking? What fears do they have?
- Assess your leadership team. Does it include former outsiders or people who interact regularly with outsiders? If not, consider how the composition of the team might be adjusted.
- What training should be provided to the three critical volunteer teams—small group leaders, children's ministry volunteers, and welcome/hospitality team members—to raise their awareness and sensitivity to outsiders?

PERSPECTIVE 10

Look Up Before You Look Ahead

"**L**eaders gaze across the horizon of time, imagining the attractive opportunities that are in store when they and their constituents arrive at a distant destination."* This quote from *The Leadership Challenge,* one of the classic books on the subject, accurately describes the way that most of us think about leadership. Leadership is future oriented. It is positive. It creates movement.

I have referenced this quote often, and I still believe it to be true . . . to an extent. Leaders do need to look ahead and move their churches or ministries toward a more vibrant future. But the thought of overcoming all the barriers to change, as described throughout the preceding perspectives, can seem overwhelming from a human perspective. That is why looking ahead isn't a leader's first job.

Your first and most important job is to *look up before you look ahead.* You need to look to God for guidance, wisdom, and strength before embarking on a journey of change. And you need the other leaders around you to do the same.

I will get straight to the bottom line of this chapter. If a church or ministry's leaders are not genuinely seeking God and praying, "Thy will be done," their change efforts have little chance of succeeding. Without this kind of selfless spiritual posture, the debates about how to proceed will inevitably devolve into contests of "*My* will be done."

---

*   James M. Kouzes and Barry Z. Posner, *The Leadership Challenge: How to Make Extraordinary Things Happen in Organizations* (San Francisco: Jossey-Bass, 2007), 17.

147

And "my will" often translates into the path that is most comfortable or most beneficial for those at the decision-making table.

The members of Grace Church were proud of their many mission partnerships. The chair of the mission council enthusiastically said, "We have so many different partners that you can't list them on a single sheet of paper." But the church's leadership team had a growing awareness that the large number of partners was spreading the church too thin. After a thoughtful discussion, the leadership team decided to identify a small number of outside ministries as the primary focus for the congregation's mission work. The other ministries would not be eliminated, but the selected ones would receive more promotion and resources.

The conversations went well, and the leadership team seemed to be reaching a consensus, until the time came to select the specific core mission partners. When a preliminary list was proposed, one member of the team became visibly agitated: "I can't imagine why we would leave the prayer blanket ministry off this list. That group has been knitting and delivering blankets to our community hospital for over twenty-five years. It's one of the best things we do." A different person responded, "I value that ministry as well, but its impact is nothing like these others. Are you more sensitive about this since your wife leads the prayer blanket team?"

You may not have had this conflict, but you've probably encountered something similar. No one on the leadership team will say they don't want God's will to guide their decisions. Agreement may come easily as long as the conversation stays at the conceptual level. But when the time comes to make concrete decisions, the tension between "thy will" and "my will" often surfaces.

A variety of factors contribute to a "my will" mentality. Sometimes a person's strong preferences cloud their judgment. Or long-held patterns and habits prevent them from seeing any other possibilities. Sometimes, as in the previous example, a leader is advocating for a spouse or friend who is not in the room. Wrapped around all these factors is the possibility that spiritual maturity is lacking among some of the people at the table. This can hinder both that leader's and the group's discernment as they pursue God's guidance in the conversation.

This is not to suggest that God's will is always counter to an individual's desire or that leaders will easily agree on the direction in which God is leading their church or ministry. One of my favorite Bible verses is the letter from the Jerusalem council that reports, "It seemed good to the Holy Spirit and to us" (Acts 15:28). The letter was written after a heated debate about whether to impose Jewish practices on new gentile converts. Even the most prayerful, God-seeking individuals will have different perspectives at times, especially around decisions that represent major changes.

The story in Acts also offers a caution for leaders who are committed to looking up before they look ahead. If a church's major decisions never create tension, leaders may have settled for an easy answer, even a good one—but not necessarily a Spirit-led one. Their variation on the Acts passage may be something like, "It seems good to us, and we hope the Holy Spirit will agree."

If this rings true, you may wonder how your church got to this point. It is a church, after all, so seeking and following God should be the norm. But regardless of how you ended up in this place, the more important question is how to reverse a pattern in which genuinely praying "*thy* will" is a struggle. What are the practical ways that you can begin to look up before looking ahead?

The Answer Begins with You

Whether your role is lead pastor, associate pastor, another staff position, lay leadership, or the director of a faith-based nonprofit, you need to lead the way. It is simply not realistic to expect a leadership team to go to a deeper spiritual place than you have gone yourself.

How would you describe your spiritual disciplines? Do they include reading Scripture, meditating, listening to God in prayer, and other means for being drawn into God's presence? Are these practices vibrant or perfunctory? Are they a vital part of your day or something you squeeze in when you have time? When faced with major decisions, do you spend more time in prayer or in analysis? When life gets hectic or stressful, are your spiritual practices the first thing you turn to or the first to go?

This is vitally important for two reasons. First, whatever God is doing in your life will leak out. If you are experiencing God's presence in life-giving ways, people will notice. Similarly, if your comments about following God are not coming from the depths of your soul, those words will sound hollow to the people you are leading. The former inspires people to go deeper in their own spiritual lives, but the latter makes them wonder why they should read Scripture and pray. The former gives weight to your words while the latter just raises questions.

There's a second reason "looking up" needs to start with you. This chapter addresses the problem of putting "my will" over God's will in the corporate life of the church. But pastors are not immune to this problem. Effective ministry leadership requires a fine balance of confidence and humility. When leaders become too confident, they tend to leave God behind, working from their own strengths and pursuing their own agendas. What if the path that you're pursuing sounds like a good choice but isn't God's choice? The best way to escape this trap is to foster an active spiritual life.

Grace Church would never have begun the conversation about focusing its mission work without the prompting of their pastor, Zach. The leadership team knew Zach took one day a month for a personal retreat. He had explained to them that this was an important way for him to refresh his soul and stay connected to God. On more than one occasion, Zach had met with the leadership team after a retreat day and said, "Here's something I'm sensing from

God. I'd like us to discuss it and see what you're hearing." When Zach told the team he believed God wanted to produce more fruit from a smaller group of mission partners, no one doubted that this was the outgrowth of a season of prayer by their pastor.

The inner work that leaders need to do to keep their focus on God is the subject of entire books and is well beyond the scope of this chapter.* But let me close this section with a personal appeal. If you've sensed a nagging feeling as you've been reading, it may be a gentle nudge from the Holy Spirit. Don't ignore it! The practices that connect you to God and enable you to look up are far more important than any other leadership tool or perspective in the rest of this book.

The Answer Doesn't Stop with You

Pastors play a vital role in leading their churches to look up before looking ahead, but they can't do it on their own. It must be a team effort. Unfortunately, people are often asked to serve in volunteer leadership roles without enough consideration for their spiritual maturity. Ruth Haley Barton says, "One very common leadership mistake is to think that we can take a group of undiscerning individuals and expect them to show up in a leadership setting and all of a sudden become discerning!"[†]

No church intentionally sets out to place undiscerning individuals in leadership roles. But inadequate screening and selection often result in this outcome. When that happens, it's not surprising that decision-makers struggle to pray "Thy will be done" for the

---

* Three of the books on this topic that I recommend most often are Tod Bolsinger's *Tempered Resilience: How Leaders Are Formed in the Crucible of Change* (Downers Grove, IL: InterVarsity, 2020); Ruth Haley Barton's *Strengthening the Soul of Your Leadership: Seeking God in the Crucible of Ministry* (Downers Grove, IL: InterVarsity, 2008); and Reggie McNeal's *A Work of Heart: Understanding How God Shapes Spiritual Leaders* (San Francisco: Jossey-Bass, 2003).

† Barton, *Strengthening the Soul*, 198.

congregation; they don't have enough personal experience with the same prayer.

Does this description sound like your church or ministry? If so, keep in mind that you didn't get here overnight. It is a pattern that developed over the years, perhaps long before you arrived. Entrenched patterns won't be broken quickly, but they can be changed with intentionality and patience. Your awareness of the problem is a first step, but creating a commitment to pray "thy will" requires a change in how the congregation thinks about leadership. The best tools for shifting the congregation's thinking are your communication about leadership decisions and the selection process for new leaders.

Each time you speak or write about an important decision, you have an opportunity to reinforce the desired practice of seeking and following the Spirit's guidance. This applies to future decisions and ones that have just been made. Your leadership team's decisions should reflect your best understanding of God's will, so explain this clearly to the congregation. Grace Church didn't simply narrow the number of mission partners in order to use resources more efficiently. Zach and the leadership team prayed about it and believe that they are following God in this decision.

This kind of communication creates an expectation within the congregation: "We're prayerful as we make decisions. Our leaders are praying 'thy will be done.'" Of course, this assumes that leaders are truly seeking God in their decisions. That leads to the second tool—the selection of people to serve in leadership roles.

Every congregation or ministry has a process for choosing people to fill official leadership positions, such as board members and committee chairs. An expectation for God-seeking decisions should influence the criteria for evaluating and selecting those leaders. Too often the criteria emphasize leadership in the workplace, length of time in the church, and size of financial contributions more than spiritual maturity.

Rather than a résumé-driven process, questions around spiritual depth and spiritual leadership should become primary. Of course, it is impossible to truly assess someone's spiritual maturity, and it may even feel judgmental to try to do so. But if you aren't intentional about incorporating the spiritual dimension into the selection, the process will default back to the factors that are more tangible and visible.

The responsibility for choosing leaders may rest with the leadership team or a nominating committee or staff. Regardless of who is involved, you can begin a conversation with them about the selection process. Separate the discussion from actual selections so that it doesn't appear that you're trying to disqualify a potential candidate. Talk about the ideal evaluation criteria and how these compare with what has been done in the past. Allow time for them to discuss concerns, such as "How can we know if someone is spiritually mature?"

Of course, you can't know about someone's spiritual qualifications with certainty. But you can ask questions that provide insights. Ask about their spiritual practices or how they seek God's guidance for important personal decisions. Invite them to tell you about a person who has been a spiritual mentor for them, or about someone they are mentoring or shepherding in the faith. Asking these kinds of questions will influence the selection process and will eventually reshape the leadership team.

The same kinds of questions should also be asked of anyone who is being considered for a staff position. The tendency to focus on visible qualifications can be even more pronounced in hiring practices than in choosing volunteer leaders. Think about the interview questions for your most recent hire. How many of those questions addressed past experiences and training, or the person's "fit" with the current staff and culture? Compare this to the number and depth of questions asked about their interior, spiritual lives. You may discover a need to make some adjustments.

This kind of screening—for volunteer leaders and staff—is not the only step to consider. The churches and ministries that are most serious about leadership selection go much further. Some create formal apprenticeship programs for potential members of the leadership team.* Others require anyone in a key leadership role to be in an intentional disciple-making relationship.

Wherever your leaders are on the path toward spiritual maturity, you can create an environment that encourages looking up before looking ahead. This is especially important if you're faced with the prospect of waiting several years for more mature people to be placed in leadership roles. One of the best ways to create this environment is in the design of meetings for your board or leadership team.

Change Your Meetings

Meetings are not a popular or energizing topic. Everyone has experiences with meetings that are boring or a waste of time. In some cases, advocacy for "my will" turns into ugly and ungodly conflict. But you can't avoid meetings; the decisions that will shape your church or ministry's direction are made in these gatherings. The important question is how to make your meetings more meaningful and reflective of a "thy will" mindset.

What was the last meeting of your board or leadership team like? Think about the agenda and the discussions in that meeting. Did you focus on the right issues? In what ways did the group listen for what God might be saying? If the only spiritual moments were a cursory prayer at the beginning and end, then you shouldn't be surprised at a less-than-spiritual outcome. Meetings that look very similar to those of secular organizations will lead to business-oriented decisions.

If you're serious about listening to God, then be serious about it in your meetings. You can do this in a variety of ways, starting

---

* Phil Taylor's *Eldership Development: From Application to Affirmation* (Orlando, FL: Floodlight, 2017) offers one example of this process from screening through the entire training/apprenticeship cycle.

with expanding the role of prayer within the leadership team. When weighty issues are being considered, the team can stop and spend time praying about the decision. They can divide into smaller groups to pray with one another. If the matter isn't urgent, they can even postpone the decision until the next meeting and ask everyone to pray for clarity on how to proceed.

Waiting until a subsequent meeting to decide can be a powerful way to reinforce the message of listening to God. Businesses have rigid agendas and schedules for making decisions, but the Holy Spirit doesn't operate on a human timeline. When a leadership team hears, "We need more time to pray about this decision," it's a reminder that they are not in a corporate or political process.

That is exactly what happened as Grace Church tried to finalize their core mission partners. The disagreement over whether to include the prayer blanket ministry threatened to upend the entire process as other members of the leadership team began asking about additional missions that were not on the list. The chair reminded everyone of the reasons that they had agreed to focus on a few core partners. When one team member suggested that they should vote on the list that had been proposed, Zach jumped in and said, "We don't have to decide tonight. I'd rather table the discussion so that we all have more time to pray and reflect on this."

A reliance on prayer and a willingness to wait are two important ways of building a greater reliance on God in leadership meetings. Steering away from traditional votes is another element, as highlighted in the story from Grace Church. Taking a vote, in which a simple majority decides the outcome, is a political process that seems devoid of the Spirit's presence. It is far better to work toward a consensus so that a leadership team can say, "It seems right to the Holy Spirit and us." Consensus does not necessarily mean unanimous support, but it is much more robust than having 51% support for a proposal.

The example from Grace Church also points out the perspective that leaders need to bring into meetings. They should not think of themselves as advocates or representatives of an interest group, like the leadership team member who was protecting the prayer blanket ministry. Instead, leaders need to listen to God and to one another in order to make the best decision for the church. It is a posture that leans toward God and away from self-interest. Many leadership teams have long-established patterns of special interest advocacy, so this posture calls for unlearning old habits and learning new ones.

Leadership teams that listen to God in their decision-making set the tone from the start of their meetings. Rather than jumping into the business at hand, they might ask someone to share their faith story or invite the group to share ways that they experienced God's presence that week. They might read and discuss biblical narratives of leaders who sought and followed God's guidance, even when it didn't "make sense." Demonstrating that the spiritual agenda is just as important as the rest of the agenda can help any leadership team pay closer attention to where God is leading.

I led a strategic discernment retreat for a church that was at a major crossroads. It had been a sleepy community church for decades, but in the three years before the retreat, they had experienced dramatic growth. While growth is exciting, it brings its own challenges around physical space and programming. The tension within the team was growing as they debated the pros and cons of different options. Suddenly, a door opened and the youth choir entered the room, singing a beautiful worship song. It was a divine interruption that reminded all of us why we were there.

Change the Culture

Perspective 2 looked at the powerful role that culture plays in facilitating or hindering change. This chapter is essentially a deep dive into the most important change that can be made in a church's culture. When the leaders and the members of a church are serious about praying "Thy will be done," God does amazing things.

The book of Acts describes one Spirit-led cultural change after another. The council of Jerusalem, mentioned earlier in this chapter, was a watershed culture change as church leaders proclaimed that gentile believers were not required to follow certain practices of the Jewish faith as a prerequisite to being a follower of Jesus. But this isn't the first or last major culture change in Acts.

At the end of Acts 4, a culture that valued its possessions turned into one of radical generosity. After Stephen was stoned in Acts 7, a Jerusalem-centered culture became geographically dispersed. Peter's vision and encounter with Cornelius in Acts 10 catalyzed a shift from a kosher culture to one without dietary restrictions. Paul's vision of a man in Macedonia opened the door for the gospel to penetrate one new geography and culture after another.

These culture-changing moments were only possible through the power of the Holy Spirit. Left on their own, the human change agents—Peter, Paul, the church leaders in Jerusalem—would most likely have stayed within the boundaries of what they knew from their former beliefs.

Left on their own, your leaders and congregation will also tend to stay in the familiar waters of what is known and comfortable. The same is true for you. If you don't believe this, think about how often your plans for the future use words like *better* or *improve*: "This step will improve our children's ministry" or "Our music will be better with these changes." These words, and the related actions, indicate incremental changes to what currently exists.

I am not against making improvements, nor am I saying that God wouldn't lead a church to do ministry in better ways. I am not even saying that making incremental changes is easy. I am saying that "improving" may not be sufficient to revitalize a congregation and make meaningful strides toward God's preferred future. And when "better" is not good enough, stepping into the unknown, outside of your congregation's collective comfort zone, is a Spirit-led endeavor.

The message of this chapter is about a change within the change journey. It's about the essential change in spiritual posture that must precede any kind of significant directional change. When leaders genuinely say and pray "Thy will be done," the door is opened for God to move the church toward an exciting new future. Don't let the apparent simplicity of looking up before you look ahead keep you from realizing the power that can come from making this change. It's the last perspective in this book, but it's the most important change you can make.

FROM PERSPECTIVE TO PRACTICE

LOOK UP BEFORE YOU LOOK AHEAD

- Identify one spiritual practice that you need to add to the rhythm of your life. Put something in place that will help you turn this into a habit. For example, tell a close friend, leave a reminder note in a place where you'll see it, or set an alarm on your phone.
- What is your assessment of the overall spiritual maturity of your leadership team(s)? Invite other trusted leaders to make their own assessments and then discuss this question as a group.
- Meet with the chair of your board or leadership team to evaluate the most recent meeting based on the ideas in this chapter. Then create the agenda for the next meeting, focusing on ways to raise the spiritual temperature and allow more space for the Holy Spirit to work.
- Meet with the group that is responsible for selecting leaders to discuss how spiritual depth can best be considered in the selection criteria and process. Do this at a time when you do *not* need to fill any positions.

AN *Artist's* PERSPECTIVE

When Is a Work of Art Finished?

How does a composer know when the musical score is complete? How does a painter decide to put down the brush? How does a sculptor know when the sculpture is finished? The reality is that an artist's work will never be perfect, but at some point the labor must stop. The difficulty, for artists and for leaders, is knowing when to step away and be satisfied with a job well done.

Leonard Cohen's hit song "Hallelujah" took five agonizing years to write. An early version of it was rejected by his record label, so he went back and continued refining it. In fact, the version of the song that is best known today was revised by other singers and didn't become a hit until 15 years after Cohen first recorded it.[*]

Artists can, and should, step back and evaluate their work from time to time. How else will they know if the proportions of the central figure in a painting are not quite right, or if the build in the music fails to create the desired energy? Often, stepping back means putting down the brush or pen or chisel for a day or two and then coming back with a fresh perspective. This discipline of critiquing and refining is essential for artists; there will always be something that can be made even better. An equally important skill is knowing when to stop.

---

[*] Carly Mallenbaum, "Why It Took 15 Years for Leonard Cohen's 'Hallelujah' to Get Famous," *USA Today*, November 11, 2016, https://www.usatoday.com/story/life/music/2016/11/11/leonard-cohen-hallelujah-jeff-buckley/93632656/.

This tension is particularly palpable for sculptors working with marble or other kinds of stone. Their work is done by subtraction, not addition. The statue emerges as they wield their chisel. But too much "improvement" can result in disaster. If they continue to chip away in the name of betterment, the would-be statue will become nothing more than an expensive collection of marble chips.

Pastors and ministry leaders should always pursue excellence in whatever they do. Just like the artist, they need to step away and evaluate whether their tentative plans are ready to be unveiled to the public. Sometimes they will discover that more work needs to be done. But they also need to remember that perfection is an unachievable goal and that putting the final touches on a plan is just the starting point for change.

The Courage for Change

If leading change is an art, then leaders are artists. You may not think of yourself as an artist, but the conclusion is inescapable. You, along with other leaders, are trying to create something new. You may have been inspired by examples of other churches or ministries, but your creation will be unique to your context. You pray that your work impacts countless lives, but you don't have an instruction manual, and you can't predict the outcome. Doesn't that sound like an artist?

Creating a piece of art is an act of courage. Actually, the act of courage comes in displaying a new piece of art to the public. Regardless of the form of art, the artist spends hours toiling over their work in private, trying to get it just right. Then the moment comes to show it to the public, and the artist holds their breath waiting for a reaction. What will people say? Will they love it or criticize it? Will they see the deeper meaning?

Think of a huge debut—the premiere of a major movie or the release of a highly anticipated novel—that will be the subject of reviews in the national press, countless blogs, and online ratings. It is a courageous act for these artists to allow their creations to be judged by thousands or millions of people they don't know. It's an equally courageous act for an unknown artist to show their work to a handful of family members and friends they do know. In either case, the possibility of rejection is real, and the pain that could accompany this rejection is high.

As a leader, your work is like that of an artist. Some people will appreciate the creation that emerges from your change leadership, while others will be critical. But there is also an important distinction.

The fans and critics of an artist must wait for the final product, but people can critique your leadership before the outcome is known. They have a front-row seat and can offer comments and opinions at every step along the way. Can you imagine someone disagreeing with a painter's choice of brush rather than waiting to see the painting? And yet change leaders deal with similar challenges every day.

The perspectives that form the core of this book will help you turn some critics into supporters. Or at the very least they can soften the intensity of the opposition and give you the resolve to push through the resistance. The ten perspectives show ways to build a more robust leadership team so that you can make wiser decisions and weather seasons of conflict. But regardless of how well you apply these lessons, there are two things they cannot do. They cannot guarantee successful outcomes for your change efforts, and they cannot eliminate criticism.

Leading change always involves risk, uncertainty, and pain. The last perspective explored the spiritual foundation that propels a leader to engage in change, even in the face of difficulties. The work of the Holy Spirit in a leader's life is the source of the courage needed to move forward. But many leaders have a skewed understanding of courage. They equate it with charging up a hill against an enemy, despite impossible odds, even if no one is with them. In this view, courage and martyrdom are intertwined. But courage is much more nuanced than what is implied by this simplistic picture. This final chapter explores several kinds of courage you will need as you practice the art of leading change.

The Courage to Change

In writing this chapter, I wrestled with the choice of one small word in the title: "for." The chapter is about the courage *for* leading change in a church or ministry. But to lead well, you must have courage *to* be changed. Healthy organizational change will not occur unless you are willing to reflect and learn and grow and, in doing so, to change yourself.

Whether you are a young or an experienced leader, you have made a considerable "investment" to reach this point in your career. That investment includes formal education and training, time spent learning from mentors and other wise leaders, lessons from previous ministry experiences, and more. All of this has helped you cultivate a particular style of leadership. But what if some of the development that brought you to this point will not serve you well going forward? Are you willing to admit that you need to change and do the hard work of unlearning old habits and assumptions and approaches so that you can develop the new ones you will need?

Adam Grant writes, "We often prefer the ease of hanging on to old views over the difficulty of grappling with new ones. . . . Reconsidering something we believe deeply can threaten our identities, making it feel as if we're losing part of ourselves."* Learning something new—new skills or ideas or truths about yourself—may not sound threatening. But as Grant points out, it's the unlearning that is difficult.

Think about the unlearning that may be needed to leverage the perspectives in this book. A pattern of behavior may not engender trust. A way of dealing with resisters may make problems worse rather than solving them. A desire to guarantee success may prevent the launch of a promising initiative. Whether it's these or one of the other perspectives, the starting point for change is often admitting that you're part of the problem and being willing to change yourself. And that takes courage.

The courage to change can be bolstered through greater awareness of the need for personal change and encouragement from other supportive leaders. That is why the sections "From Perspective to Practice" in this book have regularly included questions for

---

* Adam Grant, *Think Again: The Power of Knowing What You Don't Know* (New York: Viking, 2021), 3.

self-reflection and for discussion with your leadership team. They are designed to open the door for discovery and insight. But you still have to choose whether to walk courageously through that door. The courage *to* change precedes all the other kinds of courage *for* change.

The Courage to Not Know

One of the hardest phrases for a leader to utter is "I don't know." This is especially true for pastors, whose formal training prepares them to *know* the answers to complex theological questions. While theology shapes and informs leadership decisions, it doesn't provide all the answers.

Ron Heifetz and others offer an important distinction between technical and adaptive challenges[*] and the leadership required for each. For a technical challenge, the solution is known because someone has already figured it out. The optimal number of children in a classroom or the skills needed to be an effective small group leader are technical questions. Adaptive questions do not have known solutions. Becoming a church that serves and reflects the neighboring community is one such challenge. Leaders may see hints regarding how to address the question, but adaptive work always takes them into unknown territory.

Significant change will always be more adaptive than technical. Think of any of the bigger challenges facing your church or ministry. If the solutions were obvious, you'd already be implementing them. But adaptive issues defy easy answers. This reality puts leaders in the position of not knowing the best path forward. And for leaders who pride themselves on being able to answer every question, this is a very uncomfortable place to be.

What is your mental model of an effective leader? Is the ability to answer all questions and offer clear direction an important part

---

[*] The concept was first presented in Ronald A. Heifetz and Marty Linsky, *Leadership on the Line: Staying Alive through the Dangers of Leading* (Boston: Harvard Business Review, 2002).

of that ideal image? Some leaders would rather bluff than admit not knowing the answer. Even if you are comfortable saying "I don't know," your congregation may not be ready to hear it. Within every congregation and ministry, some people put leaders on pedestals, expecting them to be closer to God and therefore better prepared to confidently and accurately declare where God is leading them.

Saying "I need help" is closely related to saying "I don't know." This is much more than asking for assistance with a task, such as "I need help setting up chairs." The more difficult request for help relates to making decisions. If you don't know how best to reach and serve the church's neighbors, then you need a team that will prayerfully discern a path forward and lead the implementation. Unfortunately, some leaders view asking for this kind of help as a sign of weakness. They ignore the proverb that "plans fail for lack of counsel, but with many advisers they succeed" (Prov 15:22).

In truth, neither statement indicates a leadership deficiency. They are simply a leader's admission of being human. No one person is supposed to have all the answers or be able to single-handedly lead an organization. We all know this in our heads, but a variety of pressures and prevailing stereotypes make it difficult to utter the words. Nevertheless, if you want to master the art of leading change, you need to have the courage to say "I don't know" and "I need help."

The Courage to Invite Differing Opinions

Saying "I don't know" is done most easily in a cozy gathering with a few trusted friends. But pastors and ministry leaders may need to voice these words in larger gatherings that include people who are skeptical or critical of them. That takes courage. It takes even more courage to reach out to these less-than-supportive individuals, seeking their input or inviting them to be part of a leadership team.

One of the threads running throughout this book is that change is not a solo endeavor. It takes a team to make wise decisions and to lead the new initiatives. The easy path is to recruit a group of like-minded friends who may offer minor input but who would never seriously disagree. But this shortcut is unlikely to produce optimal long-term results. The best teams bring diverse talents and perspectives to the table, which means including people who don't see eye to eye with you.

Think of two or three people whom you are reluctant to invite into a leadership position, despite the fact that they have clear leadership gifts. What is your hesitation? If these individuals lack spiritual maturity or they behave disruptively, then listen to your instincts and leave them on the outside. But if your reluctance is just because they see things differently or because they ask a lot of questions, they may be exactly the people who need to be in the leadership circle.

As you think about these individuals, ask yourself, "Will we make better decisions with these people at the table?" "Do they bring a valuable perspective that would otherwise be missing?" Having these people in leadership roles may result in better decisions and broader congregational support. This conclusion may seem obvious while calmly reading a book, but it can be difficult to reach out to people who challenge you. Just remember that "resisters are not the enemy" and that this courageous step can open the door for your change efforts to take root and have greater impact.

The Courage to Fail

Change based on tactical questions tends to produce small, incremental nudges with a good chance of success. Adaptive questions often result in major shifts with unpredictable outcomes. This is an oversimplification, but it illustrates an important point. Victory is never assured when leading significant organizational change. Therefore, the courage to fail is an essential attribute for change leaders.

Many leaders, and the people they lead, operate from a risk avoidance perspective. They want a sure bet. They may give lip service to a notion such as "failing forward," acknowledging the growth that is possible when setbacks occur. But then they quickly ask about a proposed change, "Will this succeed?" The question often points to a fear of failure that can undermine change efforts before they ever get off the ground.

How should a leader respond when people want assurance of success? One temptation is to confidently say, "Of course it will work," even when you have doubts. This response holds the critics at bay for a while. Another temptation is to back away from the proposed change and find a path that is safer or less conspicuous. Wise leaders sometimes start with a smaller, less visible experiment, as we saw in perspective 7, but only as a step toward bigger changes.

When a major change is the best path forward and the outcome is not guaranteed, what should a leader do? The better and more difficult response is to acknowledge the uncertainty and step out in faith anyway. This should not be seen as an excuse to skip the hard work of planning and preparation, but it is a recognition that, even with your best efforts, the desired results may not be achieved. Leading and leaning into this possibility of "failure" requires courage.

Failure is in quotes in the previous sentence for a reason. Our scorekeeping culture focuses on visible results, and creating useful metrics is an important tool for leaders. We certainly need to evaluate the fruitfulness of a change. But what if success is also defined as obedience to the leading of the Holy Spirit and the learning that comes from the change? Discovering what works is valuable, but so is learning what doesn't. In this sense, an initiative that doesn't achieve the desired outcomes may still be seen as a win.

A desire to avoid failure can also lead to the mistaken conclusion that inaction is the best option. If a major change could "fail," then is doing nothing the "successful" option? That seems to have been the perspective of the third steward in Jesus's parable of the talents (Matt 25:14–30). That steward received a single talent and did not lose the money. He returned every penny that he was given—after burying it in the ground—but his risk-free approach was condemned as poor stewardship.

Failure is never easy. Nothing I write will change this reality. But this brief section will be a "success" if it helps you reframe your understanding of failure and, in doing so, gives you more courage to lead change.

The Courage to Persevere

Do you remember the "ice bucket challenge" in 2014? It required a kind of courage to stand still while having a large bucket of ice water dumped on one's head. But it was a grit-your-teeth-and-get-it-over-with courage. The unpleasant part was over in seconds.

Leaders might be more willing to try bold change initiatives if this same kind of courage was all that was needed. But as we have seen, organizational transformation is a slow process with many twists and turns. It is the opposite of the ice bucket challenge. It requires a different kind of courage: the courage to persevere.

Too many change efforts have failed because of a lack of perseverance. It takes courage to keep going when the initial results are disappointing. It takes courage to persevere when a critic seizes on the moment to proclaim, "I told you this idea wasn't going to work." Or even worse, "I told you this leader wasn't going to work." It takes courage to press ahead when supporters abandon their commitment to a task—or worse, their commitment to you.

This is not to say that leaders should press ahead with every change effort, regardless of opposition, warning signs, and disappointing results. The art of leading change involves distinguishing between an experiment that isn't going to work and an initiative that needs a little more time and support. On the surface, they may look very similar. But in one case, leaders need to pull the plug and learn from the experience, while in the other case they need to make adjustments and press ahead.

Perseverance, by definition, has a long time horizon, which makes this kind of courage particularly difficult to maintain. Courage leaks, and a depleted reservoir of courage can be catastrophic for a change effort. You don't need persevering courage to step under a bucket of ice water because it's over in an instant. In contrast, change usually gets harder before it gets easier, which means even more courage is needed 6 or 12 or 24 months into the process.

The courage to persevere requires regular replenishment of a leader's courage reservoir. Jesus's life suggests that communing often with the Father, withdrawing periodically from the work of ministry, and receiving support and encouragement from friends are all vital practices that can restore a leader's courage. Entire books have been written on the rhythms and practices that enable spiritual leaders to stay connected to God and lead in healthy ways. I will simply close with a reminder that all the other forms of courage described in this section will not produce lasting change if leaders lack the courage to persevere.

The Courage to Leave

An office building may have a universal key that fits all locks, but a "universal leader" exists only in myths. Leaders are called to a specific role and context. Said another way, your gifts may be just what a church needs in one season, but not in the next one. Some leaders get so comfortable in a context that they miss the Spirit's promptings. It can be especially difficult when leaders sense a nudge to leave but have no idea where they will go.

Leaders should not expect their tenures to be short, but they should be willing to leave when they sense, after discerning with the help of the Spirit, they are no longer the right person for the role. Just as organizational change calls the people in a church or ministry out of their comfort zones, vocational change calls a leader to do the same. Staying and persevering require courage, but so does leaving.

Even when it seems like God is opening a new door, the decision to leave is often not clear-cut. Leaders may create long lists of pros and cons for the new opportunity. They may receive conflicting advice from people they trust. They will almost certainly feel many different emotional tugs. And just like so many other decisions in leading change, whatever they choose will be questioned by some people.

A leader's decision to leave often begins with hearing a gentle whisper. Of course, some leaders maintain such a frantic pace that they can't hear anything quieter than the roar of a jet engine. Your starting point may be to slow down and listen to what God seems to be saying in the deepest parts of your soul. If you hear a whisper calling you to start a new chapter, pay attention. It often takes time, prayer, and wise counsel to discern whether an impulse to leave is driven by frustration or fatigue or the Spirit. But if you know that God is calling you to close the current chapter, you can also be confident that God has a plan for you and the church you're departing. And that should give you the courage to leave.

The Courage to Lead

"Are leaders born or made?" The question has been asked for years, and my answer is "Yes, both." Some people are born with incredible leadership gifts that are evident before they reach adulthood. Others are not "born" leaders, but they grow into significant leadership roles through training and experience and reflection. And of course, Scripture is clear that the Spirit gives the gift of leadership to some. Regardless of whether a leader is born or made, the act of leadership requires courage.

You could ask the same question about artists: born or made? In a similar way, the answer is that both are true. Regardless of the skill they had when they entered the world, you won't find successful artists who don't work at their craft, learning and experimenting and developing new abilities. And if an artist lacks the courage to show their work to the public, you will never hear of them.

You may be early or late in your leadership journey, in the first chair or some other role, in a context that challenges you every day or in one that brings you constant joy. Wherever you are, take a page from the artist. Pick an area where you want to grow, and then be intentional to learn and experiment and develop. Allow God to shape and use your leadership to build a more vibrant church or ministry. Know that you can't produce a masterpiece every time you touch the canvas of leadership. But also know that nothing will happen if you never touch that canvas. And if you find yourself gripped by fear as you begin to take that step, remember the words of God to one anxious leader: "Be strong and courageous. Do not be afraid; do not be discouraged, for the Lord your God will be with you wherever you go" (Josh 1:9).

Acknowledgments

I know that only a few people read a book's acknowledgments—mostly the ones who hope to see their names and a brief word of gratitude. The problem I face in writing these acknowledgments is that this book is the product of hundreds of conversations with pastors, ministry leaders, volunteer leaders, seminary faculty members and students, and others. I can't possibly name all the different individuals who have shared their stories and shaped my ideas about leading churches and ministries. But I can start by saying thank you to each person who has allowed me to be their consultant, leadership coach, learning community facilitator, seminar leader, or conversation partner. My understanding of leadership, my writing, and my life are richer because of my interactions with you.

Even though I can't name everyone, I can single out a few people who have been instrumental in moving this project from the seed of an idea to fruition. Greg Ligon and Jared Roth gave valuable input on the first draft of the manuscript, pointing out rough spots and gaps that I needed to address. Tom Billings did the same, and he challenged me to take a deeper dive into the book's art motif and my treatment of science versus art. David Maldonado graciously gave me perspectives through an artist's eyes, which I certainly needed, since the last time I dabbled in visual art was in middle school. Tod Bolsinger, Lisa Greenwood, Matt Steen, Phil Taylor, and Don Underwood provided encouragement when I was uncertain about the merits of the project and my initial set of perspectives.

One of the most important places where I continue to gain fresh insights are the peer learning groups that I am privileged to facilitate for Texas Methodist Foundation and other entities. These high trust environments create the space for participants to have genuine conversations about their leadership successes and failures. I am grateful

Acknowledgments

to TMF for giving me these incredible opportunities and indebted to each of the participants in these groups.

I am also grateful to the team at Fortress Press for seeing the value not only in this project but also in two of my previous books that they have relaunched. Scott Tunseth, my editor, has been a great sounding board and wordsmith to shepherd this work to its final version.

I strongly believe we are called as followers of Christ to be part of a local community of believers. I'm thankful to be part of a vibrant, healthy body at City Church in Houston. Leo Schuster, our pastor, and Valerie Tompson, our executive director, along with the rest of the staff and leadership team, make it a joy to serve in ministry there.

During the pandemic, many of us became more aware and more appreciative of classroom teachers (among other professions). In the early years of my pathway from STEM student to engineering to business, I would never have guessed that I would write a book. But the seeds were planted in those years, thanks to the investment of three high school English teachers. They are all part of the great cloud of witnesses now, but I am still grateful that Geraldine Castleman, Jane Mitcham, and Natalie Huckabee showed a math and science nerd that words could be as powerful as numbers. To any teacher who picks up this book, know that your work today may bloom many years in the future.

My favorite teacher is my wife, Bonnie, who is an amazing, loving partner in every part of my life. She didn't flinch when I told her about this book, even though she knew the time it would take, and she has been an incredible encourager and supporter every step of the way. I'm also blessed by our children—David and Karlie, Matthew, Jonathan and Kellie, and Hope—and grandsons, Theodore and William, who inspire me in more ways than they know.

The younger version of myself never imagined writing a book, especially not on ministry leadership. In fact, my life journey is a

Acknowledgments

long list of things I never thought I'd do. As I look back, my sole (and soul) response is "Only God could do this," followed immediately by "Thank you, Lord." As I look ahead, my prayer is that I will live with a grateful heart and a commitment to wisely steward the gifts and opportunities that have been entrusted to me.

Bibliography

Barton, Ruth Haley. *Strengthening the Soul of Your Leadership: Seeking God in the Crucible of Ministry*. Downers Grove, IL: InterVarsity, 2008.

Bolsinger, Tod. *Canoeing the Mountains: Christian Leadership in Uncharted Territory*. Downers Grove, IL: InterVarsity, 2015.

———. *Tempered Resilience: How Leaders Are Formed in the Crucible of Change*. Downers Grove, IL: InterVarsity, 2020.

Bonem, Mike. *In Pursuit of Great AND Godly Leadership: Tapping the Wisdom of the World for the Kingdom of God*. San Francisco: Jossey-Bass, 2012.

Bonhoeffer, Dietrich. *Letters and Papers from Prison*. New York: Touchstone, 1997.

Collins, Jim. *Good to Great: Why Some Companies Make the Leap and Others Don't*. New York: HarperBusiness, 2001.

Collins, Jim, and Morten Hansen. *Great by Choice: Uncertainty, Chaos, and Luck—Why Some Thrive Despite Them All*. New York: Random House, 2011.

Collins, Jim, and Jerry I. Porras. *Built to Last: Successful Habits of Visionary Companies*. New York: HarperBusiness, 1997.

Edwards, Betty. *Drawing on the Right Side of the Brain*. New York: St. Martin's, 1989.

Friedman, Edwin H. *Failure of Nerve: Leadership in the Age of the Quick Fix*. New York: Seabury, 2007.

Grant, Adam. *Think Again: The Power of Knowing What You Don't Know*. New York: Viking, 2021.

Heifetz, Ronald A., and Marty Linsky. *Leadership on the Line: Staying Alive through the Dangers of Leading*. Boston: Harvard Business Review, 2002.

Herrington, Jim, Mike Bonem, and James H. Furr. *Leading Congregational Change: A Practical Guide for the Transformational Journey*. Minneapolis: Fortress, 2020.

Kotter, John. *Leading Change*. Boston: Harvard Business Review, 1996.

Kouzes, James M., and Barry Z. Posner. *The Leadership Challenge: How to Make Extraordinary Things Happen in Organizations*. San Francisco: Jossey-Bass, 2007.

Maxwell, John C. *The 21 Irrefutable Laws of Leadership: Follow Them and People Will Follow You*. Nashville: Thomas Nelson, 2007.

McNeal, Reggie. *The Present Future: Six Tough Questions for the Church*. San Francisco: Jossey-Bass, 2003.

———. *A Work of Heart: Understanding How God Shapes Spiritual Leaders*. San Francisco: Jossey-Bass, 2000.

Quinn, Robert E. *Deep Change: Discovering the Leader Within*. San Francisco: Jossey-Bass, 1996.

Rogers, Everett M. *Diffusion of Innovations*. New York: Free Press, 2003.

Taylor, Phil. *Eldership Development: From Application to Affirmation*. Orlando, FL: Floodlight, 2017.